AMERWRECKA

GRYPHON PUBLISHING
GROUP, INC.

All Profits from this Book will be donated to Charity.

DAWN OF THE GRYPHON

THE GREAT AMERICAN SOLUTION

THE AMERWRECKERS

THE GRYPHON PRESIDENCY

THE GRYPHON POSTSCRIPT

DAWN OF THE GRYPHON

THE GRYPHON PLEDGE

The World is my country, all mankind are my brethren, and to do Good is my religion. I believe in the equality of men; and I believe that religious duties consist in doing justice, loving mercy, and endeavoring to make our fellow–creatures happy.

– Thomas Paine

THE GRYPHON CREED

We hold these truths to be self-evident, that all men are created equal, that they are endowed by their Creator with certain inalienable Rights, that among these are Life, Liberty and the Pursuit of Happiness.

– Thomas Jefferson

THE GRYPHON PARTY MOTTO

Lead, Follow, or Get Out of the Way.

– Thomas Paine

CHAPTER ONE
IN ORDER TO FORM A MORE PERFECT UNION

Where is my $10,000,000 loan?

Recently a former regulator in the Government bemoaned the fact that Trillions of dollars were wasted in the most anemic, if not totally stalled, recovery since the Great Recession of 2008-2009. She made the modest proposal that it would have been better to have the Federal Reserve lend $10,000,000 to each American family rather than all of the Billions and Trillions that were lent to the banks at near zero percent interest rates. Her point was that the most conservative families could invest in ten year Treasury bonds, as the banks are doing, and earn a conservative and guaranteed two percent or $200,000 return per year. With every American family earning $200,000 per year, the recession-depression would be over. There would be no need to have 700,000 Americans declare bankruptcy each year because they could not pay their medical bills. Middle class parents would have money to put their children through college without going deeper in debt, and the next generation would not have $100,000 of student loans hanging around their neck like an anchor. With $200,000 per year, per family, no one would need to be foreclosed out of their home, and if someone "walked" on their mortgage, there would be a dozen young families ready to step in to buy the house rather than paying non-deductible rent on a small apartment.

There would also be plenty of money to pay bloated health insurance premiums caused by the President's Affordable Care Act. The "Affordable Care" Act will become the greatest example of Orwellian "Doublespeak" in the Twenty-First Century. The so-called "free-riders" who went to emergency rooms because they did not have health insurance cost American hospitals – and the American public – about $16 Billion a year. Now the President's plan according to the non-partisan Congressional Budget Office (CBO) will cost America as much as Two Trillion Dollars, or more than 100 times the current amount, over a ten year period. The CBO has a wonderful website that should be required reading for all American citizens. Along with the Government Accountability Office (GAO), there are a number of Government agencies that provide excellent reports and studies, are well run, and save the Government more than they cost the taxpayer because the analysis they do is so thorough and comprehensive. These websites give you a realistic, non-political view of the State of the Union, and the state of the Union is not good. In fact, its situation is dire, critical, and on life support.

For example, from those websites you can learn that in the President's time in office, American families have lost a staggering amount of family wealth. Starting from an average family wealth of $127,000 in 2007 to $77,000 in 2010 we are now at the 1992 average family wealth or at the time of President George H.W. Bush or Bush (41).

You could also learn from the Government websites that the Treasury Inspector General, The Honorable J. Russell George, has discovered that the IRS has distributed almost SIX BILLION DOLLARS in fraudulent tax refunds – several thousand of which went to the same address in Michigan – and if this identify theft and tax fraud is not stopped immediately, the IRS's negligence will cost the American taxpayers more than TWENTY BILLION DOLLARS over the next five years. Therefore, according to a report from the Government and Treasury Inspector General George – a report that is available on the Internet – the IRS's inability to stop tax-refund fraud is actually a larger problem than lower income people going to hospital emergency rooms without insurance.

Not only did America lose its benchmark "AAA" status last year, average income and median income for working families has gone down over the past ten years. The percentage of Americans who are able to work, but cannot find work, is at an all time low – nearly 61%. Forget the often unreliable unemployment rates published monthly, because many people have either not applied for unemployment benefits or stopped looking for work altogether. Moreover, disability payments have soared as a new form of "unemployment" compensation.

The only thing that has steadily gone up is the poverty rate, which, at over 15% is the highest it has been since the war on poverty began in 1963. Just like the war on drugs, it appears that "Poverty" has won the war – with 50,000,000 Americans now living below the poverty level, with no health insurance, and without opportunity or hope. Clearly, this terrible state of affairs is not the President's fault. Unfortunately, his policies have not helped, and in many cases, his policies have actually exacerbated the problems. His was to be an administration of Hope and Change, but instead the poverty and unemployment suffered by the Black, Hispanic, and other minority communities is in the high double figures of 21-25%.

The Black and Hispanic communities voted overwhelmingly for the President, and yet this President has conducted more raids on "illegal" Mexicans and deported more Mexicans than all of the other Presidents in American history combined. No one ever hears of "illegal" Canadians being deported.

This year, for the first time in history, the wealth of the average Canadian family has actually surpassed the wealth of the average American family. Obviously, we need the Keystone Pipeline more than the Canadians need us and fairly soon, the Canadians will close their borders to us, their poor neighbors to the South. Senior citizens will need to sneak across both borders to get the prescription drugs they need at a price they can afford. A good example is the notorious Boston criminal Whitey Bulger who, while hiding from the Government for his murders and crimes in Boston, was able to regularly cross the border into Mexico to get his prescription drugs. The President's Justice Department is unable to capture and prosecute the "Whitey Bulgers" of the World, but look at the number of young black men incarcerated by this President just in Boston for only using marijuana or other party drugs that the President himself admitted to using. Poverty, unemployment and crime are all up in Black America, all the while the President bailed out the big banks and Wall Street without concern for Main Street, the Black Community, or our Mexican brethren to the South.

The President believes that income redistribution is the solution. The real solution is to make sure that "opportunity" distribution is available to all. The money that the President wasted on bailing out

Wall Street and even bailing out General Motors could have been used instead to send every Black and Hispanic teenager in America to a prep school like the ones Mark Zuckerberg or Bill Gates attended. It is interesting to note that "prep school" prepared both Gates and Zuckerberg so well they could each confidently drop out of Harvard without a second thought. Conversely, the drop out rate of inner-city Black and Hispanic students is at an all time high. Recent Government statistics show that if you graduate high school, graduate college, get married, stay married, and have children after you graduate from college, you have a 91% chance of success to become a successful American middle class family.

To the contrary, if you follow the path of most Black and Hispanic young people today by dropping out of high school, never going to college, never getting married and having children before graduating from high school, your chances of success in America are an abysmal 4%. Winning the lottery will change your circumstances, but not make you a better person. Going to a classic New England prep school or one of the new charter schools around the country will change a young person's life, but the President has provided no money to accomplish that goal because much of his support comes from the entrenched status quo of teachers unions. As strange as this might seem, if you are Black, Latino, or of Hispanic background and you care about your family or even your family back home in Mexico, you cannot afford to vote for the President.

My Friend, this book is written for you. Pretend it is the Christmas season of 1776. America is about to be born. You are poor, hungry, cold, sick and sleeping outdoors in the cold and wind. You are here to fight and die for your family's future. The Government does not care about you and answers only to the aristocracy and the plutocracy that really run the country. Today, everything is great for the people at the top – and the people at the top rig the game by utilizing the Federal Reserve, the big banks, and even Wall Street itself so they can keep winning at your expense. And if they lose every once in a while, they turn their private speculation into massive public debt under the theory that they are "too big to fail." The plutocrats and the aristocrats control both parties and all branches of the Government. If you really want to change things, you must stand up for yourself and think for yourself. You must become like the Gryphon – have the strength of a lion and the wisdom and vision of an eagle. You must seize every opportunity because no one in the Government will give it to you.

As a citizen during the revolution, you will read tonight by the campfire *"The American Crisis"* by Thomas Paine, and in the early morning while everyone is asleep – we will cross the river together to fight for the new America and leave the old AMERWRECKA behind. If you believe in freedom, if you believe in helping your family have a better future, and if you believe that the government that governs least, governs best, it is time to join a new movement. Let us start a new revolution to make America the country that it was meant to be. Let us work together to "form a more perfect union" and STOP those who would destroy the America that the Founders and Patriots dreamed of on that Christmas Eve so many years ago, when they fought and died to protect your Declaration of Independence. You owe it to them, and you owe it to your family and future family to do what you can to make America the promised land that it was always meant to be. We are waiting for you to join us.

CHAPTER TWO
THE SEARCH FOR THE ELUSIVE "ELEKEY"

To paraphrase Winston Churchill's famous quote – or at least attributed to him – "If you are a Conservative when you are young, then you have no Heart. If you are forty, and are a Liberal, then you have no Head (or Brains)." Everyone can immediately relate to the theme, that the young are always progressive, liberal, helpful and even forgiving. As people get older, they no longer have dreams of saving the World and feeding the poor, they now want to protect their home, their families and their communities. They now have daytime jobs to worry about rather than the philosophical debates of university. Instead of homework, they now just have home and work. When they were young they were much more liberal, free-thinking and charitable with other people's money. As they grew older, they became the taxpayer and the parent and the one who had to pick up the tabs and pay the bills. Old age, parenthood, the economy, and paying the bills made them much more conservative over time.

It would be clever, but incorrect, to transpose the Churchillian quote into: "If you are not a Democrat when you are young, you have no heart; if you are not a Republican when you are old, you have no head." But America is much more complex than that. It is not enough to combine the "heart" of the Democrat's Donkey with the "head" of the Republican GOP (Grand Old Party) Elephant.

Instead, we need to create or find a new thematic political symbolic mascot that represents what is truly going on in American politics, the elusive "Elekey" that represents the best both parties have to offer and combines the best of the Republican Elephant and the Democratic Donkey.

The **Elekey**, as the perfect political beast, would of course have the "brains" of a Libertarian – totally focused on the pragmatism of the facts, the numbers, and the economy. The Libertarian does not care who you sleep with, but only cares about a strong economy, a sound dollar, America's freedoms and a live and let live attitude.

Similarly, the Elekey's "heart" would come from a Progressive, who cares about his fellow man and realizes that he must be a modern day Robin Hood that takes from the rich to provide for the poor. Both Republicans and Democrats had a "Roosevelt" that espoused such Progressive ideals.

The Elekey's "soul" would not come from the Liberal Left or the Religious Right, but instead would get its passion from the Evangelicals and its fervor and spirit from the Tea Party and Occupy Wall Street movements.

The extremists on both the Far Left and the Far Right have been marginalized by America's firm hold on the center and the politics of the possible. Above all else, the Elekey is a pragmatic beast that has a "heart" that wants to do all that is possible to do "good," but at the same time has a practical "head" that cautions we can only do so much, and that we must be reasonable in our expectations and pay our bills, no matter how passionate we are about our goals.

Currently, the Elekey is every bit as elusive as the Unicorn. But one of the purposes of this book is to introduce the new political icon for a new form of politics in America – to be called the **Gryphon** as the symbol of the newly created **Gryphon Party**. The Gryphons are both Republicans and Democrats and just as Liberal as they are Libertarian. The Gryphon Party welcomes Gays and Lesbians as well as Evangelicals. Christianity and Judaism are religions, not political parties. All faiths and religions are welcome. And just as the "Independent" and "No Labels" movements are not political parties, neither is the Tea Party. And any time someone registers as a Libertarian, the Green Party or as an "Independent," they effectively disenfranchise themselves from participating in the only two parties that really count: the Republicans and the Democrats. At least we are better than Russia, where a dozen people might run for elected office, but only a Communist Party member wins. There are so many different factions that must be appeased in both of our major American parties that the extremes of both parties result in a socially moderate, fiscally responsible centrist always winning the Presidency. The winner always makes the loser look radical, unfit, or out of touch.

The irony of this situation is that the Republicans demand that the Government should stay out of their pockets while supporting laws to look into other people's bedrooms to see who they are sleeping with or what they are smoking. Then they say they are shocked at the expense of sending a young black man to prison for 10 years for smoking marijuana, even though our past three presidents have all admitted to smoking marijuana – if not trying more serious drugs. Republicans support Capital Punishment and the War on Drugs until they realize how expensive and ineffective both of those have become.

The Libertarian "brains" of the Gryphon would argue for decriminalization of most social drugs, because the cost of prohibition has been enormous – as well as a complete failure. Similarly, the Right Wing advocates for capital punishment in California are now seeking its repeal after California has spent nearly a Billion dollars in legal fees and other costs to execute just a dozen criminals. Even life imprisonment at $40,000 a year for 50 years would amount to just $2,000,000 per criminal.

There are similar conflicts in the views of "pro-life" critics of abortion who refuse to pay higher taxes to support young mothers on welfare who have children born into poverty with no food, no money, no health insurance, and no prospects for the future as the only "education" they will receive is in the streets. The "Right Wing" combination of outlaw abortion, welfare and drugs, but keep the "death penalty" and do not regulate handguns in any way will have a dramatic and expensive impact on America's future. Our inner cities will become war zones and the only growth industry in America will be the prison industry at a huge taxpayer expense. America will cease being the land of the free and will become the land of the incarcerated and the fearful. If you think the education of the poor is expensive, just wait until you see the price you pay for their (and your) ignorance.

CHAPTER THREE
ONLY A 'RINO' CAN WIN

Another rare but essential member of the political menagerie lexicon is the RINO, or Republican In Name Only. Right Wing Republicans use this as a derogatory term to bash liberal or moderate Republicans, or even ideological Libertarians or Progressive members of the Republican Party. The obvious irony is that the patron saint of all Right Wing Republicans, Ronald Reagan, is a classic RINO in that he was a longtime Democrat, was a longtime union member, was the president of the union, was divorced, had several well known Gay friends in Hollywood, and was a two-term Governor in the most liberal state in the Country. President Reagan was always an optimist, always talked of America's better angels, and spent no time arguing about abortion, gun control, or illegal immigration. In fact, the only substantive gun control regulation of the past century, the Brady Bill, came as a result of President Reagan being shot, and the only progressive immigration reform (IRCA) and AMNESTY for 3,000,000 "illegal" immigrants came under President Reagan's administration. It is almost comical to see candidates like Newt Gingrich praise President Reagan now, when during the 1980's Gingrich accused him of wrongdoing in the Iran-Contra affair and incompetence in reaching out to Gorbachev and Russia during the height of the Cold War. Instead of being the Right Wing's patron saint, Ronald Reagan was in reality one of history's classic RINO's. The same is true with Reagan's successor, President George H.W. Bush, or as we refer to him: Bush (41).

"Little else is requisite to carry a state to the highest degree of opulence from the lowest barbarism but peace, easy taxes, and a tolerable administration of justice; all the rest being brought about by the natural course of things."

– Adam Smith

Before he dies, hopefully someone will tell President George H.W. Bush or Bush (41) that history will prove that he was the best President of the Twentieth Century. The years of prosperity and peace that America enjoyed from 1992-2000 were all because of the "reasonable" and "rational" policies adopted by President Bush (41) during his term of office from 1989-1993. The "budget deal" that he created with Senator Bob Dole, which is criticized by current Republicans, is what created America's prosperity and the only balanced budgets in the past 50 years from 1996-2000. Others will claim credit for the peace, prosperity and balanced budgets of those years because success has many fathers while failure is an orphan

(JFK comment on the Bay of Pigs fiasco). But history will show that President Bush (41)'s policies solved the great recession of 1991, the Savings & Loan crisis, the first war in Iraq, and a number of other national and world problems without bankrupting the nation by fighting needless wars and lowering taxes on the wealthy. In the 1990's, Americans and the Middle Class flourished. Since the election of President Bush (41)'s son, Bush (43), the essential Middle Class in America has been victimized and eradicated. The American standard of living has gone down for ten straight years, median income has decreased, and the average family wealth has been nearly cut in half while poverty, joblessness, and the uninsured have all increased dramatically. The Government bureaucracy, and the corresponding deficit, has grown so large that even if we were to confiscate the **entire wealth** of the 400 wealthiest Americans, those Americans that the IRS monitors each year to see how much they – the top 400 – are paying in taxes, it would not even pay one year's interest on the national debt of SIXTEEN TRILLION DOLLARS. The national debt does not include the over SIXTY TRILLION DOLLARS of unfunded liabilities for future funding of the "Safety Net" of public benefits such as Social Security, Medicare and Medicaid. Therefore, both sides are correct.

The anti-tax people are correct to say we do not have a "revenue" problem – we have a spending problem. The Government payroll must be cut. But we cannot pull the "Safety Net" of benefits out from under Americans in need during this, the worst economic crisis since the Great Depression. Just as President Nixon exclaimed that "We are all Keynesians now;" so, too, should we now admit that we have also become Rawlsians – as in John Rawls, the Harvard Social Scientist known for his writings on the "Safety Net" and why it is an essential part of modern society, as well as the "promise" that is the social contract between a government and its citizens. More than 50% of all Americans count on the "Safety Net" for their very survival.

Now we come upon this critical juncture in American history where the very fabric of the "Safety Net" is being stretched and torn in ways not previously imagined. Millions of the working poor and even former employed members of the working class are falling through the "Safety Net" as never before. People are still losing their homes in record numbers. Americans on Food Stamps are at an all time high. The uninsured constitute well over 50,000,000 Americans or roughly one in six of the population. Each year, over 700,000 Americans declare bankruptcy because of uninsured medical costs.

The President has been unsuccessful in solving any of these problems, because he has increased the deficit and increased the bureaucracy in Washington, which is increasing the problem as opposed to finding the solution. Now that former Massachusetts Governor Mitt Romney has emerged as the eventual Republican nominee and the President's challenger in the November 2012 election, the President's supporters will do their best to paint Governor Romney as a radical social conservative because they know America is thirsting for change, but no Democrat will vote for a hard-core social conservative. Instead, what most Americans want is a fiscal conservative that is also a social moderate that only a RINO can provide.

The truth be told, every one of the Author's Republican friends was an early Romney supporter. Romney has a lot of support among Independents and Democrats in the business community who realize the President has put America on the wrong track and the consequences of a second term will be dire. As for me, I was a Huntsman supporter and was disappointed that he left the race so early.

Even more surprising, my wife and I as life-long Republicans, – along with our formally liberal, now Libertarian daughter –

all voted for the President in 2008 (See recently published collection of essays entitled "Why We Left the Left," by Tom Garrison, including "Old Enough to Know Better, Still Young Enough to Care"). My wife and daughter were staunch Hillary Clinton supporters (and they still are); while I was a John McCain supporter, until he chose his running mate. In retrospect, picking Senator Joseph Lieberman would have been a brilliant choice, as well as the real **"Game Change"** referring to the book and the excellent movie of the same title.

America needs a new "Era of Good Feelings" that it has not had since President Monroe's tenure in office as the fifth President of the United States. America cannot afford four more years of partisan squabbling, but America will vote for the President unless Governor Romney proves that he is, in fact, a RINO; if he cannot make it all the way to being a full-fledged American Gryphon. To defeat the President and position himself to save America as the next President, Governor Romney must do three things:

1. Get the vote of young, unmarried women;

2. Get the vote of a majority of Hispanic-Latino voters;

3. Pick a credible Vice President that no one could question.

If Governor Romney does these three things, he will be able to win in November – and if as President he reads the rest of this Book, he will be able to put America back on the right track. So let us examine these three strategies as well as addressing the must-win "battleground" states of the Electoral College and making several good recommendations for a potential Vice Presidential running mate in order to avoid the same mistake Senator McCain made.

The President's supporters have already delivered the votes of older working women, working mothers, and stay-at-home mothers by attacking Ann Romney and suggesting that as a mother – "she never worked a day in her life." This was a political blunder of the first magnitude. By all accounts, Mrs. Romney is a wonderful woman and an excellent mother and parent. She is also Governor Romney's better half and best spokesperson. She is a warm and generous person that is suffering from the disabling disease, multiple sclerosis. Even the Mafia does not go after the other guy's wife and kids. Attacking Mrs. Romney gets Governor Romney halfway home with the women's vote. Now he just needs to divorce himself from the hard Right Wing of the Republican Party that complain about the Government being in their wallet – but feel that it is the Government's job to police the morality of young women and regulate their access to birth control. There were so many stupid, crude and inappropriate comments made by numerous members of the "Neanderthal" Wing of the Republican Party that there is no wonder that the President enjoys a huge lead among young women. Too many young women are rightly worried that old white men with grey hair – or even worse – fat and bald misogynists – will control their future, invade their bedrooms, and limit their access to prescription drugs such as birth control. Men should not come between a woman and her doctor – at any time – period. But how ignorant do you have to be to think the President could do anything about a woman's access to birth control or even an abortion if she wants one?

I have met people who are "Pro-Life" or "Pro-Choice," but I have never met anyone who is "Pro-Abortion" or "Anti-Life." Even assuming the next President stacked the Supreme Court just to overturn *Roe v. Wade,* 410 U.S. 113 (1973), what good would that do? *Roe v. Wade* is just based on *Griswold v. Connecticut,* 381 U.S. 419 (1965), which would return "abortion rights" to the individual states – just like capital punishment or other laws and regulations left to the states including health insurance mandates. So assuming *Roe v. Wade* was overturned at some point in the future, all that would do is allow the individual state legislatures to limit abortion or reproductive rights. So for every Arizona or Utah that would pass a law limiting abortion, there would be states like California, Oregon, New York and Massachusetts that will not change their current laws at all. So a new law in Arizona prohibiting all abortions would just cause young women to move to California or New York, or fly to Europe. That is if they can afford to travel. If not, the poor young woman – especially if she is a minority – would be forced to have the baby and if the baby was not adopted, she would be on public assistance for the next 18 years and have the "Neanderthal" critics call her a "welfare queen" or even worse language for a situation that is really not her fault; certainly not entirely her fault.

Assuming that once Governor Romney wins the nomination, he will start acting like the former Governor of Massachusetts instead of an ultra-conservative talk show host, he should do just fine with young women and undo the damage done by the less intelligent members of the Republican Party's Right Wing. Also assuming that they let Mrs. Romney play a prominent role in the campaign, Governor Romney will do just fine with the women's vote.

Similarly, once he has the Republican nomination sewn up, someone should advertise the fact that Governor Romney is a first generation Mexican immigrant as his father was born in Mexico.

With all of the fuss over the President's birth certificate, you would think that 40 years ago people would have made a big deal out of George Romney being born in Mexico. **None** of my friends who are ardent supporters of Governor Romney knew that his father was born in Mexico. I cannot imagine that given a choice between the current President and his administration, that have set the all-time record for deporting Mexicans and launching immigration raids on innocent workers, that a person who is exactly like them – the son or daughter of a **Mexican** immigrant father – that the Hispanic-Latino vote will not go to Governor Romney in overwhelming numbers, once that little known fact goes public.

The Women's vote will be important in all 50 states, but the Hispanic vote will be critical in several crucial battleground states like Florida, Colorado, New Mexico, and Nevada. If you review the Electoral College scoreboard with the states that the President won (365 Electoral votes) versus the states that Senator McCain won (173 Electoral votes), and then look at the individual states that are leaning toward the President or against the President; one can start changing the potential score of the Electoral College, which is what the November election results will be based on regardless of the overall popular vote.

The best guide as to what states Governor Romney could or should win that Senator McCain lost is to analyze the states that voted for Bush (43) over Senator Kerry in the election of 2004. In the 2004 election, President Bush (43) won 286 Electoral votes over Senator Kerry's 252. With a total of 538 Electoral votes at stake, 270 is the key number. Each state that goes for Governor Romney in 2012 that went for the President in 2008 reduces the President's lead and adds to the Governor's count, so based on the 2008 Electoral College results where the President had 365 Electoral votes and Senator McCain had 173, there are certain states that will certainly go Republican Red and other states that will go Democratic Blue. Moreover, if Governor Romney just gets the **exact same** states that President Bush (43) did in 2004, he will win 286 to 252.

Bush (43) won key battleground states like Virginia, North Carolina, Ohio (the key state in 2004) and Florida (the key state in the 2000 election). If Governor Romney only wins Ohio with 20 Electoral votes, Florida with 27 votes, and North Carolina with 15 votes, that is 62 Electoral votes that the President loses and his challenger gains. If Governor Romney just wins his three home states of Michigan, Massachusetts, and New Hampshire, those are critical states that neither Senator McCain nor Bush (43) won. Governor Romney could win all of New England, but for purposes of this discussion let us assume that we only give Governor Romney Michigan with 17 votes. There are many pundits that say Michigan will go with the President because of the General Motors/UAW bailout. Governor Romney's father was a very popular two-term Governor and one of the original "car guys" that made Detroit famous. Michigan will go for Governor Romney.

Similarly, Indiana with 11 votes, Minnesota with 10 votes, and Wisconsin with 10 votes will go Republican because of strong Republican governors, public union issues, and right-to-work state issues that will favor Governor Romney. Iowa with 7 votes is already leaning for Governor Romney, and Bush (43) won Iowa. That leaves the Hispanic-Latino voters in Nevada (5 votes), Colorado (9 votes) and New Mexico (5 votes). If they go for Governor Romney, then he will have the McCain states of 173 plus 136 Electoral votes from the states listed above for an Electoral College win of 309 votes over the President's 229.

So what could go wrong? The President has a slight lead in the battleground states of Ohio (20 votes), Florida (27 votes), and Wisconsin (10 votes). But Bush (43) won Florida and Ohio over Senator Kerry; John Kasich is a very strong new Republican Governor in Ohio; and Governor Romney will win the Hispanic-Latino vote in Florida once his family history comes out that he comes from a family of Mexican immigrants. However, even if we give Wisconsin back to the President, he still loses the Electoral College 299 to 239.

To insure that Governor Romney wins, he needs to choose a successful former Governor as his running mate and future Vice President – someone who is eminently qualified to be President and someone that is attractive to Independents and cross-over Democrats. For that reason, Governor Huckabee, the former Arkansas governor is a perfect choice, especially to get the Jewish vote because of his strong support of Israel. But Arkansas, the Deep South, the Evangelicals, and the Religious Conservatives will all vote against the President. Similarly, Governor Huntsman is the best Republican Conservative on paper, but Utah will already vote for Romney, as will all the Mormons in the Western states like Nevada and Idaho. Governor Huntsman is an excellent candidate for the future and would make an excellent Secretary of State because of his experience as the Ambassador to China.

There are three popular former Republican Governors that make sense for Governor Romney to choose as his running mate: George Pataki – former governor of New York, Tom Ridge – former governor of Pennsylvania and first Secretary of Homeland Security, and Tom Kean – former governor of New Jersey and head of the 9/11 Committee. All three are very well respected governors and statesmen.

Governor Ridge should have been Senator McCain's choice, but Senator McCain felt that he had to consolidate his "conservative" base, though it is hard to imagine anyone more "conservative" than Governor Ridge, or more well placed in the Bush (43) administration. If the Republicans spend any time talking about the A-word (Abortion), then they deserve to lose. If it is true that McCain's staff turned down Governor Ridge because he is "Pro-Choice," then Governor Romney should grab Governor Ridge with both hands because Governor Romney needs help with the demographic of younger women, and Governor Ridge can help. Governor Ridge on the ticket delivers Pennsylvania and solidifies Ohio and the "base" nationwide. Governor Ridge, as the first Secretary of Homeland Security, would neutralize the President's bin Laden "chest-pounding" commercials.

The inspired choice, however, that no one is talking about, is Governor George Pataki, the popular two-term governor of New York. If Governor Pataki is on the Romney ticket, the election will be called at 9:00 p.m. on election night. Remember, we are already giving the President California, Oregon, Washington and Hawaii. Governor Pataki would give the Romney ticket New York, New Jersey (thanks in large part to Governor Chris Christie and Wall Street workers who love Governor Pataki), New England (Connecticut and Vermont) and solidifies Ohio (Governor Kasich) and Florida (all former New Yorkers). With Governor Pataki on the ticket, Romney could win other states like Virginia and West Virginia, and solidify all of New England. If Governor Romney sweeps the East Coast from Maine to Florida, the election is over because Governor Romney will win the entire South and all of the Western states except for the "Left Coast" of California, Washington and Oregon.

Governor Pataki brings with him a huge bonus. He is a Moderate and Progressive Republican that is Pro-Choice and a strong supporter of Women's Rights and Gay Rights. Not only do Governor Pataki and his law firm Chadbourne & Parke specialize in alternative energy programs – he has started an organization that has been fighting the President's healthcare plan for several years, and his former Lieutenant Governor, Betsy McCaughey, is not only in the vanguard of women's health issues, she is a leading pundit on television attacking the President's healthcare plan. By putting Governor Pataki on the ticket, you win

New York, win the Women's vote, and win the debate over healthcare. If Governor Romney wins those three things, then he will be the next President of the United States, and he can begin the process to save America from the fiscal cliff that the Congressional Budget Office (CBO) predicts we are about to go over, while repairing the "Safety Net" for Millions of Americans, and restoring faith in America which has all but disappeared.

However, many Republicans will probably press Governor Romney to select someone more conservative to deal with the budget deficit and the impending crises that America faces with its out of control debt. Other formidable non-governor running mates that are deficit hawks include David Walker, former U.S. Comptroller General and founder of the Comeback America Initiative, and Paul Ryan, Chairman of the House Budget Committee. David Walker was actually chosen by the new internet group, America Elects, to be their presidential candidate. Walker is the consummate deficit hawk speaking out against America's national debt crisis wherever he goes. Similarly, Republican Conservatives everywhere will pound the table hard for Governor Romney to choose Congressman Ryan as his running mate because of Ryan's leadership in creating a vision not just for a new budget, but for a new way of doing business in government to stop the Country from going over the fiscal cliff in January 2013. It would be difficult to imagine anyone better suited to put the failed policies and the lack of any budget from the President and the Democratic Senate in the election crosshairs than by selecting either David Walker or Congressman Ryan as his running mate.

CHAPTER FOUR
THE AMERICAN CRISES

At the time of this writing on Christmas Eve of 2011, the overwhelming majority of Americans (85%) believe that their beloved country is on the wrong track. The other 15% do not understand the question, or perhaps just do not care. But what is wrong with America? The simple answer is its capital, Washington, D.C. Not since 1776, and the original *"The American Crisis"* by Thomas Paine, has a sovereign capital been more out of touch with its own people. Remember, George III had a much higher popularity rating in 1776 than Congress and the President enjoy now.

What is wrong with Washington, D.C.? It is the only major city in the World that has one air traffic controller in the command tower at midnight, while it has 22,000 people watching interest rates move at the Federal Reserve each day. Milton Friedman said that most of those 22,000 people at the Federal Reserve could be replaced by a computer. But humans are needed in the command tower at an airport – and hopefully more than one – lest a plane crash during a necessary bathroom break. Imagine the unthinkable carnage and horror the 9-11 terrorists could have done by taking the "red-eye" flight overnight from Los Angeles rather than the early morning flights from Boston.

This book will explore a very simple premise that just happens to be true: the more successful and important Washington, D.C. is, the more the rest of America suffers. This President, or the next President, must cut 80% of the workforce from all of those various agencies that even the Presidential candidates cannot seem to name. Virtually everyone believes that the agencies of Education, Energy, Commerce and Environmental Protection must be cut or curtailed. There is also no reason that the Treasury Department, the IRS, and the Department of Labor should not be reduced as well for reasons discussed later in this book. The President's current budget would increase the IRS's budget by over TWO BILLION DOLLARS to hire 16,000 more Special Agents to allegedly monitor his new mandatory health insurance program and audit the rich, but they will instead conduct sealed search warrant raids on ordinary Americans like you and me. But, more on that later.

Our Government employs well over three Million people, with 400,000 new jobs just added by our current President. We successfully ran the Government with only 200,000 people through World War II. The TWO MILLION EXTRA people working for the Government cost us over **$400 Billion** a year in wages, health benefits and pensions that most people in the "private" sector can only dream of – if they are in fact lucky enough to have a job. Add to this the two Million troops and "consultants" supporting them overseas in unnecessary deployments and foreign wars, and that is another $600 Billion per year. In 1960, we had less than 200,000 people incarcerated. Now, we have well over two Million people incarcerated for 10 to 20 year sentences for marijuana and cocaine, most of them black, Hispanic, and poor. It would cost far less for society to send a young black man to Harvard for four years for smoking marijuana, as the President freely admits to, rather than have the U.S. Attorney's office in Boston prosecute and convict dozens of young black men for their own future political advantage.

To incarcerate a young man in his prime – effectively putting him in a cage for 10 years and paying for his upkeep and the upkeep of his jailers and their pensions and health insurance, costs the taxpayers over $50,000 per year – or $500,000 altogether. The legal system to prosecute the young black man, who had to have counsel appointed for him, costs us, the federal taxpayers, another $500,000, for a total of $1 Million to put one young black man away on ice during his prime – when instead he could have appeared on American Idol, sung rap with Eminem, or gone to Harvard for a whole lot less; none of that would have been at our cost. What happened to the "good old days" when a young man in trouble could choose two years in the Army rather than two years in jail?

You probably have not noticed your civil rights slipping away over these past few years, but rest assured you are no longer in the land of the free or the home of the brave. Far from it. There have been more commando raids on American citizens in their homes and offices during this Administration's past three years – than at any other time in American history. This President's Attorney General referred to us as a "Nation of Cowards," yet he did not lift a finger to save Troy Davis from execution though seven of the witnesses against him recanted their testimonies or admitted to perjury. Every day the I.C.E. (Immigration Customs Enforcement) commandos storm some unsuspecting employer looking for undocumented Mexican aliens, yet not a single Islamic terrorist has been caught by I.C.E.; and to the best of our knowledge, only a couple of Canadians have been deported for overstaying their visa welcome, while this President has deported more of our Mexican friends than all previous Presidents combined.

We waste hundreds of Billions of dollars each year in bigotry and hypocrisy to our neighbors to the South that we signed a free-trade agreement with (NAFTA). We have no "trade agreement" with Cuba, but we would fight to keep Elian Gonzalez here against his father's – and Castro's – wishes. Yet there are several Republican candidates who are seriously considering deporting all 12-13 Million "illegal" Mexican immigrants home when their only "crime" seems to be mowing Mitt Romney's lawn. There were no Mexicans hijacking the planes on 9-11, and though 19 of the 21 hijackers had Saudi passports, we have spent the past decade fighting wars in Afghanistan and Iraq. Our "Shock and Awe" campaign against Iraqi cities should have been directed to the mountains of Tora Bora in Afghanistan. It turns out that Osama bin Laden left Afghanistan years ago – and so should have we. As for the war in Iraq – Secretary of the Treasury Paul Snow and Counsel of Economic Advisors Larry Lindsey were asked to leave George Bush (41)'s cabinet when they questioned the cost of the pending war in Iraq at over $200 Billion. Now, years later, there are books titled *"Fiasco"* or even *"The Three Trillion Dollar War."* Suffice it to say, we have clearly wasted America's time, treasure, and youth on a war that can only be called a big mistake. There never was any "good" reason for the war in Iraq, and it has clearly added $3-4 Trillion to our already bloated national debt.

But even without the unnecessary deployment of our troops all over the World and the unnecessary wars, we would still have a deficit of over $10 Trillion. We do, in fact, have a deficit of over $16 Trillion on its way to $17 Trillion. If our interest rates go from 2% to

7% as Spain and Italy's have recently – all of our tax revenues will go to just one thing: paying the interest on our National debt. That is it. No Social Security, no Defense spending, no Medicare or Medicaid, just the interest on the National Debt.

Therefore, taxation is not the issue, but immediately cutting Government spending is. If 80% of the bureaucrats working for the thousands of agencies that no one can remember were cut, the 4,000 new laws and regulations just passed were all repealed or suspended, and the tax rates of 10%, 25% and 35% were made permanent, then America would have a balanced budget in no time. The Stock Market would soar, home building and sales would increase, there would not be any cuts in public welfare or Social Security or Medicare as savings could be realized there as well, and we could even keep a few military bases in England and Germany for American soldiers to visit now that they no longer need to die in the deserts of Iraq or Afghanistan. Our energy problems could all be solved without foreign oil; our healthcare could be free; and our health insurance voluntary, not mandatory, and at affordable rates. Is this all fantasy? Not at all; these are all realistic solutions to where we find ourselves now in the "American Crises." The premise is simple: if you vote to re-elect the President, there will be no way to save our great country. This will be the most important election of your lifetime, no matter how old you are.

That is what this book is about. We must change directions before it is too late, and we become like Greece, Italy, or Spain. There will be rioting in the streets and the "Occupy Wall Street" movement will be a fond nostalgic memory. When taxes, food, energy and healthcare costs use up every dollar of income, there will be no customers to buy things. Without customers, there will be no jobs. No jobs means no tax revenue for Washington. Two thousand wealthy Americans are giving up their American citizenship each year, and Social Security will now be **out of money** in 2033 instead of 2036. That is only 20 years away, less than one generation from now. Make no mistake, the "Safety Net" for us all has been stretched to the breaking point and if something is not done soon – by everyone – we will all be responsible for the collapse of the greatest nation on Earth.

THE GREAT
AMERICAN SOLUTION

CHAPTER FIVE
TRUMPED

Love him or hate him, Donald Trump has turned his name and personage into one of America's most emblematic business icons. Whether in television, real estate, his properties, his golf courses, or even in his new perfume, "The Donald" has "Success" written all over him. So how did Mr. Trump go from respected American business icon to "carnival barker" in the matter of a week when he was contemplating running for the Presidency because the President was doing such a "horrible" job and the Republicans were not putting forth a credible candidate?

There is no question that Donald Trump is an extraordinary businessman and dealmaker; the record speaks for itself. He might even be a good President someday, but he lacks the political savvy to get elected. In other words, he has a penchant for telling the truth, as blunt and hurtful as that might be; and he does not lie or hide his true feelings. Unfortunately, that trait can be fatal to a modern politician.

So what was Trump's big mistake? He unwittingly fell into the media trap of speaking about the President's birth certificate, as if most Americans care about that issue. After making just a few comments questioning the legitimacy of the President's birth in Hawaii, Mr. Trump found himself in the unusual position of being ridiculed, if not totally subject to abject scorn. In the space of a week, he went from being considered as a possible Republican or Third Party candidate for President to just another political hack shooting his mouth off, and no one wanted to come to his Presidential debate.

How could this have happened? Mr. Trump made a classic mistake in thinking that the American people really cared where the President was born. Just because certain right-wing conspiracy theorists thought they could unseat the President by proving that he was born in Kenya, or some place other than Hawaii, that does not mean that anyone would care or have standing to get the issue into a federal court. The truth is that if the President could solve the problems of the Country including unemployment, the economy, and the price of energy, people would not care if he was born on Mars. Trump, the businessman, miscalculated. Just as Trump the businessman would borrow from the Chinese instead of the British to save 50 basis points on a loan, so, too, the American people would vote for a Martian that could end the two needless wars, increase employment for all, provide for the poor without overtaxing the middle-class, and solve the problems caused by the Great Recession.

Trump did very well during the Lost Decade from 2000-2011, but very few others did. Real wages were down, food and gas prices were up dramatically, unemployment was up, and the stock market was down. Median wages actually declined over that period. Median family wealth was almost cut in half to 1984 standards, and health insurance premiums went up 120% during that time period. A whole generation approaching retirement saw their 401k's and pension plans wiped out by bank fraud and mortgage frauds that they did not even understand. If you spend all of your time on television holding court over a primetime slot or in a golden palace on Fifth Avenue, it is difficult to imagine how many people in America are suffering: the 50,000,000 people without health insurance, the 47,000,000 people on Food Stamps, the 60,000,000 people unemployed, underemployed or hoping for a better job.

Trump also forgot that more people voted in American Idol than in the last Presidential Election. For a man that prides himself on having his finger on the American pulse, that is an unforgivable sin. How could such a smart businessman be so clueless? Having done very well for himself in the Cult of Personality that dominates American reality television, it is understandable that he plumb forgot that most Americans are looking for real solutions to their real-world problems, from which Mr. Trump has never really suffered.

Americans were looking for a savior in 2008. The President has the chance to be either remembered as Jimmy Carter (one failed term) or FDR (two terms to transform the "Safety Net"). Mr. Trump had already made up his mind that the President was a failure, without regard for the fact that 45% of the people believe that the President is doing a good job and 45% of the people would vote for **anyone** other than the President, even for Donald Trump perhaps. But of that 45%, only a small percentage of the group cares about the President's birth certificate or if he is a Muslim. Assuming that 90% of the 45% that would vote for **anyone** but the President do not care, or about 40%; and we can add to that the 10% that are not paying attention or legitimately have no opinion, add to that the 45% that genuinely like and support the President, and you now have 95% of the American people feeling that Trump has taken a wrong turn and has totally missed the boat in underestimating the American public's desire for change for better, real world solutions, and not more television or fantasy political rhetoric. So it was very easy for the President to dismiss Trump as just another political hack crying out in the wilderness – or just another "carnival barker" trying to get the attention of the American people.

The American people know they have problems, and they are looking for someone to save them. If not the President, then perhaps

Donald Trump, but the American people are looking for someone to save their future – to literally save their lives and the lives of their children. The President does not have the answers or the solutions, and half the population believes that he is the "clueless" one and has the country on the wrong track. We will never know if Mr. Trump has the answers and the solutions because he questioned the birthplace of the President and effectively relegated himself to the "basement" of American politics where they hide the political "carnival barkers" that embarrass both parties. If Mr. Trump could critique himself on a new show "The President's Apprentice," he would probably say: "What a great guy. I truly respect him – very smart guy, but he made a big mistake and had to be fired."

So let us start our own political rumors. Governor Romney was born in Mexico and is an illegal alien that wants to run for President. This is the total truth. The problem is – it is the truth about the 1968 election where no one made a big deal of Governor George Romney's Mexican heritage or birth outside of the United States. Governor George Romney was a very popular two-term Michigan Governor who promised to stop a very unpopular war among other populist promises. No one asked to see his birth certificate.

The truth is that Mitt Romney is a first generation Hispanic immigrant that has done well for himself and his family just as so many other **first generation** immigrant Americans, whether they be from Mexico, Cuba, Germany, Ireland, Italy or Lithuania. Their families came to America for a better way of life. Blessed be the America that immigrants risk their lives to come to – and count yourself as fortunate if you were lucky enough to be born here. America still needs a savior, and the chances are overwhelming that our next President will be the son of an immigrant. America, as a nation, was built by immigrants and has benefited by the new ideas and new companies created by immigrants.

So what about Donald Trump? He can still save America. Maybe not as President, but we definitely need more Donald Trumps in America. Every state and city either has a Donald Trump or needs one. America needs the Donald Trump of the Wollman Rink in Central Park. All of the money in New York could not get that Rink up and running. But once Donald Trump put his money, support, and reputation to work – the Rink was fixed, open, and operating – even more beautiful than in the past.

The states and the cities should give properties that they have taken over to the Donald Trumps of America – for free – and with tax advantages for the future so that old buildings can be demolished and replaced with new buildings and new tenants. Rules can be set in place that most of the properties must be rented to low-income families and only 10-20% can be sold or rented to the affluent. If America is always building, then Americans will be at work. If Americans are at work, America will have full employment. We need the Donald Trumps to keep doing what they do best, make deals and keep America building and working – especially in real estate, affordable apartments, and home building.

America needs more Donald Trumps and fewer regulations. We need more building and less taxes. If we stop growing, we stagnate and die. America needs more immigrants, more young people, more jobs, more building, and less regulation and less taxation. The more successful the Donald Trumps are, the better off the rest of America will be. In the final analysis, we do not need Donald Trump as President; we need him and others to keep the wheels of business turning as successful entrepreneurs and leave the job of President to the sons of immigrants.

CHAPTER SIX

THE DECLARATION OF ENERGY INDEPENDENCE

Prior to the election of 2012, it is anticipated that Americans will experience the most expensive gasoline prices of all time. Already Americans are spending more on food and energy than at any other time in American history. The price of gasoline has almost doubled from $1.95 a gallon when the President took office in January 2009 to over $3.80 a gallon in February 2012. The price of gas is well over $4.00 a gallon in many parts of the country, and may touch $5.00 a gallon before the November 2012 elections, unless America falls back into recession.

At the time these words are being written, the President has already blocked the Keystone pipeline project despite its many obvious advantages, and the President has applauded the passage of the payroll tax cut so Americans could afford to fill up their gas tanks for Memorial Day and the Fourth of July.

America's energy crisis is a self-inflicted wound. We overtax our fellow Americans by Trillions of dollars to fund needless wars fought in desert territories where the locals despise us and where we cannot trust our supposed allies to lift a finger to help us. We let hedge fund managers speculate in oil as if it was like soybeans or pork bellies, instead of the lifeblood of our economy. When margins were raised on trading silver, the price of silver dropped from $48 per ounce to the low $20's almost overnight. It has taken months for silver to crawl back to the low $30's, only to fall back into the mid $20's again.

Similarly, the price of natural gas has plummeted from approximately $7.50 per Mcf (1,000 cubic feet) to $2.50, to even below $2.00 per Mcf for the first time this year, while a barrel of oil has hovered between $95 and $105 per barrel. There are 42 gallons of gasoline made from a barrel of oil. Without getting into the difficult math of converting the energy production as measured in BTUs – British Thermal Units – of a barrel of oil that will later become 42 gallons of gasoline or heating oil after being refined, suffice it to say, that 1,000 cubic feet of natural gas (Mcf) delivers about 17% of the energy of a barrel of oil, or about six units of natural gas for each barrel of oil. So, assuming that we find oil at $100 per barrel, we would need six units of natural gas to equal the BTUs of a barrel of oil – or 6,000 cubic feet at $2.50 per Mcf, or $15 in natural gas terms to replace the energy of a $100 barrel of oil. Thus, assuming a ratio of six units of natural gas to one barrel of oil, the cost would be between $12-$15 for natural gas to replace each $100 of a barrel of oil that we use for heating our homes or running a power plant. Significantly, America is the Saudi Arabia of natural gas, but imported oil is literally killing us and driving us deeper and deeper into collective bankruptcy.

Many promoters of natural gas say that they need natural gas to return to the old price levels of $7.50 before it is a sustainable investment to "drill for" and invest in, which would mean $35-$45 for enough natural gas to replace the traditional $100 barrel of oil. But right now there is a glut of natural gas in America, and it has been determined that we have 300 years worth of natural gas just in America. Don't worry, a discussion of drilling in Alaska is coming up next, but if we are the "Saudi Arabia" of natural gas, why are we not converting everyone's oil burners to natural gas, and why not convert all utilities to natural gas or nuclear power? Why not have all Government vehicles, all city buses, and all large trucks required to run on liquefied natural gas? Saudi Arabia has publicly acknowledged that they **must** keep the price of oil above $90 per barrel to pay for all of the public welfare programs that they have promised their people. But in America, because of the current **glut** of natural gas, the price has plummeted from the high seven dollar range to below the two dollar range. Forget wind and everything else, why wouldn't the President support natural gas drilling everywhere, the Keystone project, and any other American natural gas drilling projects? He promised as much in his January 2012 State of the Union speech. His actions, however, have absolutely crushed the price of natural gas since then, and raised the price of foreign oil. As far as our trading partners are concerned, the President's "actions" speak much louder than his words.

If the President was truly serious about allowing increased drilling in America, it would not have cost Shell Oil over **FOUR BILLION DOLLARS** just for EPA approvals and environmental studies to drill offshore from Prudhoe Bay, Alaska, which has been the most successful source of oil production in North America. No one pays income taxes in Alaska, except for the "seven sisters" oil companies. Instead, each Alaska citizen receives an annual dividend distribution from the Permanent Fund that is a multi-Billion dollar fund created by the drilling from Prudhoe Bay.

Moreover, the Alaska Pipeline created hundreds of Millions of dollars in jobs and incomes for young people from all over America that flocked to Alaska, just as Americans now flock to North Dakota for jobs or could have flocked to the Keystone project had the President not scuttled the building of the new pipeline to let energy flow from the oil sands of Canada to the refineries in Oklahoma and Louisiana. Prudhoe Bay also provides a healthy dividend-paying stock for income-starved investors listed as BPT on the NYSE that pays a fairly consistent dividend of about 8%, or $8.00 per year at about $100 per share based on oil production and royalty payments from the production of Prudhoe Bay.

Drilling just in the areas where we know there are great treasure troves of oil can turn the tables on OPEC and change our energy dependence into energy independence. If only the American people understood the great wealth lying underground and underwater in Alaska, while Millions in America go cold in the winter and stay at home in the Summer because of the price of oil.

So why have the great Alaskan oil reserves not been tapped? Environmentalists have run out of logical excuses, and if the President and members of Congress cared more about the American people and less about the migration and mating habits of the caribou, the drilling would have already started in the Arctic National Wildlife Refuge in (ANWR) and the National Petroleum Reserve in Alaska (NPRA). The Alaskan people – and especially the Alaskan Native Communities – all favor drilling in Alaska. Even the caribou love to make homes near the Alaskan Pipeline to keep warm. But it is the American people in the lower 48 states that are ignorant of the immense size of Alaska, the relatively microscopic size of the typical drilling site, and the incredible wealth that ordinary Americans could enjoy from the renewed drilling in Alaska.

To understand the immense size of Alaska, imagine if you could pick up Alaska from an old flat Mercator map of the World. If you placed Alaska and its islands over the Continental United States, it would stretch from California to South Carolina and take up virtually the entire lower 48 states. If you cut out from your imaginary map California, Texas and Florida, Alaska could cover the entire Continental United States, as Alaska covers 425,000,000 acres of land.

The regions that we are talking about drilling in ANWR and NPRA have 19,287,000 acres and 23,500,000 acres, respectively. Yet, certain people in Washington, D.C. would rather spend Trillions in fighting needless wars in Kuwait, Iraq and Iran to protect the Straits of Hormuz for the Saudis, rather than open up the tremendous wealth of Alaska to protect what – the caribou?

As it stands now, Prudhoe Bay has about 1,100 oil wells on 213,500 acres. The fighting is all about opening another 2,200 acres for drilling. Downtown Houston is only about 1,200 acres and has just one oil company, a small oil company, Callon Petroleum which is developing the 8,800 acres that it owns in the Texas range known as the Permian Basin. The Permian Basin in Texas is approximately 240,000 square miles (800 miles by 300 miles), which means that it is 153,600,000 acres, at 640 acres per square mile. Therefore, just the Texan Permian Basin is larger than the entire state of California, which is a little over 100,000,000 acres in size.

The site in ANWR that oil companies would like to open up for new drilling is only about 2,200 acres out of 19,000,000 acres in ANWR, and 425,000,000 acres in Alaska. As a point of reference, the Ted Stevens International Airport in Anchorage is about double that space, at 4,800 acres. Arguably, no one in Washington, D.C. would care if the Anchorage Airport doubled in size to 9,600 acres – so why the fight to prevent drilling in ANWR or new drilling in Prudhoe Bay or off the coast of Barrow?

So now that you are imagining that Alaska is bigger than the Continental United States minus Texas, California, and a few other outlying states; and that the famous fertile oil ground of the Permian Basin in Texas is actually larger than the State of California; let us consider Death Valley National Park in California. Death Valley grew by 1,200,000 acres to a total of 3,336,000 acres and was designated a national park with the passage of the Desert Protection Act of October 31, 1994. But of the 3,336,000 acres in Death Valley National Park, well over 3,000,000 acres is pure, undeveloped desert wilderness. There is nothing at all in the 3,000,000 acres of desert wilderness, and what people think of the actual park itself that tourists go to is a much smaller area. Is there any doubt that if gold or oil was discovered on the Death Valley property that it would have been developed – or mined – rather than be left as desert? For an answer to that question, one need only look at upper class neighborhoods in California, like Huntington Beach, that have small active oil wells all over town.

Now, assume that oil was discovered in Death Valley, enough to transform the California economy from its near-bankrupt state to a wealthy oil producer the size of Norway or Venezuela, and worthy of OPEC membership. Imagine that you can get all of the oil that you want from the 300,000 acres that are already somewhat developed and you will leave **untouched** the 3,000,000 acres of pristine desert wilderness. How would you vote? Now, how would you feel if some East Coast senators from small states were blocking your state from financial surplus and full employment? Remember, in Alaska there is no income tax or sales tax. There are only royalty payments by the big oil companies to the Permanent Fund for the citizens of Alaska to receive annual dividends.

What if we just thought of the property that has been abandoned by the Government in the Continental United States, known as "Brownfields?" The Government Accountability Office (GAO) estimates that there are approximately 425,000 Brownfield sites throughout the United States. Brownfields are industrial sites that have some sort of environmental pollutant problem or chemical hazard such as oil, paint, or other dangerous chemicals that makes the land toxic or unusable. The GAO estimates that there are over 5,000,000 acres of **abandoned** industrial sites just in our nation's cities. This is roughly the same amount of land occupied by our 60 largest cities. Remember, downtown Houston is just about 1,800 acres. This is land that we have voluntarily abandoned and refuse to use or develop for anything.

As part of the Brownfields reclamation project, the Government can require that the abandoned sites that receive Government grants for cleaning up the sites use the money to facilitate the building of new energy sources, including green energy and alternative fuels. For example, an abandoned Army base in Arizona or Nevada can have acres and acres of solar panels and wind turbines to create new sources of power for the surrounding communities. Even if not competitive at first, over a period of three to five years, the projects will pay for themselves, and then the next twenty years the project will be producing abundant amounts of low cost, clean, and renewable energy from abandoned environmental waste sites.

America already has 5,000,000 acres of abandoned land that no one is trying to reclaim or save. New oil wells in just 2,000 acres of ANWR can help to end our energy dependence on countries that are actually hostile to us.

As mentioned above, the famous drilling spot in Alaska, Prudhoe Bay, on the North Slope, has 1,100 wells on 213,500 acres. We are willing to leave 3,000,000 acres undisturbed in Death Valley. Arguably, the most beautiful – and the most famous of the National Parks – Yellowstone National Park, has only 2,219,789 acres in total. I say "only" because we could carve eight or nine "Yellowstone's" out of ANWR and NPRA to keep as "wilderness" and no one would notice the land we opened up for drilling. We only foresee 200,000 acres for drilling in each of the Alaskan preserves and no one would miss the land or even see the oil wells from any of the new "national parks" established in ANWR or NPRA. And remember the current fight is over only 2,200-2,500 acres for drilling. Also, please remember that NPRA stands for National **Petroleum Reserve** in Alaska. What are we waiting for?

It is also important to note that Yellowstone Park is bigger than several East Coast states, including Delaware and Rhode Island combined. In 1988, wildfires destroyed over 800,000 acres of

Yellowstone, or an area the size of Rhode Island at 793,880 acres. So, if Mother Nature could destroy 800,000 acres of one of our most beautiful National Parks without Congressional action, and we have already abandoned 5,000,000 acres of Brownfields, then why would Congress not answer the prayers of all Alaskans, and most Americans, to just open up 200,000 acres in each of ANWR and NPRA for oil drilling? After all, the National Petroleum Reserve was originally called the **Naval** Petroleum Reserve in Alaska to save a large source of oil for future American warships. If not now, then when?

Everyday we hear people in Government and pundits on air saying that we should open up the American Strategic Petroleum Reserve, which really was meant for emergencies like another oil embargo as happened in the 1970's, not to regulate the price of oil against hedge funds, speculators, and the Arab states in OPEC. The President could end oil speculation tomorrow by stopping the purchase of oil on margin. As previously mentioned above, just look at the price of silver in 2011 after margin requirements were increased, not once but twice. Silver is just a metal for jewelry and coinage. Oil is the lifeblood of the American economy, and the President should end the market for speculators the day after he reads this book; and before releasing any oil from the American

Strategic Petroleum Reserve, allow Shell to start drilling off Prudhoe Bay in Barrow, Alaska, and open up only 1% of ANWR and NPRA to drilling, and approve the Keystone Pipeline project.

Just as Congress has decided to auction off the airwaves to increase broadband capabilities and add to the public coffers, drilling can be opened up on national lands by having oil companies and entrepreneurs bid for the drilling rights by agreeing to pay a royalty to a Federal trust fund that would benefit all Americans, as the Alaskan Permanent Fund benefits all Alaskans. The oil companies and new oil entrepreneurs would still pay taxes – as would the Million-plus newly hired oil company employees that would be hired to work on the new oil drilling projects in Alaska and elsewhere. Cut the Washington, D.C. bureaucracy, red tape, and overly-zealous regulations and create a new Permanent Fund for all Americans. Imagine the North Dakota Bakken Shale project, and multiply it by 25 times for the amount of oil in ANWR and NPRA. With all of the excitement about the Canadian oil sands project and the Keystone Pipeline; ANWR, NPRA, and Alaskan off-shore drilling, which is all American, dwarfs any other North American project by a large multiple. Combined with the 300 years of natural gas that America has, and all of the other alternative energy options discussed in this book, the President only has himself to blame if a barrel of oil stays over $100 by November 2012.

When the President took office in January 2009, gasoline was at an average of $1.85 per gallon. In February 2012, gasoline has more than doubled to over $3.90 a gallon. This does not include state or federal taxes which make the cost of gasoline to the consumer between $4.00 to $4.50 a gallon; with premium gas hitting close to $5.00 a gallon in several areas, and by the Summer, perhaps gasoline will be $5.00 per gallon across the country unless, of course, the country falls back into recession.

The NPRA has 23,500,000 acres, or roughly the size of Maine (22,646,400 acres), and ANWR has 19,287,000 acres, which equals the rest of New England combined (NH, VT, MA, CT, RI). Barrow, Alaska is smaller in acreage – and population – than Bridgeport, Connecticut. But who would not choose to revitalize both Bridgeport and all of Connecticut (currently ranked 50th of all states in job production and job growth, as well as near the bottom of states to retire to) by allowing drilling in and surrounding Bridgeport?

There is, of course, no prospect for that happening even in the distant future, but that is not the point. No one has discovered oil in or near Bridgeport. But North Dakota has 45,248,000 acres and currently sports the lowest unemployment in the nation, a state budget in surplus, very low taxes, and prosperity everywhere because the Bakken Shale Oil Field has 6,000 active wells on only 900,000 acres. South Dakota, which has 48,000,000 acres, has several oil discoveries, all of which are smaller than the 244,000 acres marked off as the Badlands National Park. Suffice it to say, North and South Dakota have already made the decision that they will take whatever steps necessary to develop state and private lands to secure the future prosperity of their individual states.

No one in North Dakota is saying to suspend the North Dakota "payroll" or unemployment tax to allow people from North Dakota to afford the ever-increasing cost of gasoline. Once again, to put things in prospective, Prudhoe Bay, surrounding the small town of Barrow, Alaska, has only 1,100 wells on 215,000 acres, but it produces about 480,000 barrels per day and is running down. The Bakken Shale Oil Field has over 6,000 wells and is just getting started.

Similarly, while Alaska is a very large area, it only has a population of about 500,000 people. Kuwait, on the other hand, is only 11,000 square miles, where the Permian Basin in Texas is over 240,000 square miles. Kuwait has a population of 2,000,000 people, but 60% of that population is comprised of foreigners who work on the oil fields and other oil-related or menial jobs to support the ruling class. But Kuwait, as an oil-producing nation, only produces 2,000,000 barrels per day – only four times the daily production of Prudhoe Bay. While Kuwait's production accounts for only 3% of the World's output, the oil production for Kuwait and Saudi Arabia combined account for an impressive 80% of the World's excess production. The more a nation has of "excess production," the more it can export. By opening ANWR and NPRA to drilling, Alaska can match the daily production of Kuwait, and more. In 1998, the Bureau of Land Management proposed to open up drilling and sell new leases for Alaska's North Slope Borough. The proposal was to open only 600,000 acres of the neighboring 50,000,000 acres. Prudhoe Bay is already there, as is Barrow, Alaska.

Inexplicably, the Bush (43) Administration decided in June of 2005 to block the sale of the leases for no good reason. This is indeed ironic in that we have wasted more than a Trillion dollars in a needless war in Iraq, which was supposedly over oil or weapons of mass destruction. The original Iraq war, based on Iraq's invasion of Kuwait under Bush (41), cost $68 Billion, but most of this was reimbursed by willing partners that wanted Kuwait's excess production to keep flowing to Europe and the West. Almost no one supported us in Bush (43)'s fiasco in Iraq, much less reimbursed us for our Trillion dollar folly in the desert. As the President works to extricate us from the wasteful wars in Iraq and Afghanistan, perhaps he can also assure America's future prosperity by opening up the drilling in ANWR and by ordering all Government vehicles to run on liquefied natural gas with new cars and trucks produced by the revitalized – and Government owned – General Motors. No more tax subsidies for electric golf carts or windmills or Government boondoggles like Solyndra. Let's stop "crucifying" the oil companies and let them have the 2,200 acres in ANWR and expand the current offshore drilling in Prudhoe Bay.

CHAPTER SEVEN
FOURTEEN POUNDS OF SUGAR

The original title of this chapter was going to be "Fuel at Forty Cents a Gallon," but then no one would read it as being total science fiction. Truly wise and informed individuals can already guess what this chapter is all about, but what everyone in the United States, from the President on down, should understand is that it takes just fourteen pounds of sugar to make a gallon of sugar-based ethanol fuel. Forget about corn-based ethanol, which is too expensive, and forget about sugar in your local grocery store that is kept at 20 cents a pound because of government tariffs and sugar cartel pricing, and instead think about **inedible** sugar at two cents a pound. It takes 14 pounds of sugar, plus water, plus yeast to make a gallon of sugar-based ethanol that can run just fine in most modern cars.

Everyone now realizes that "corn-based" ethanol subsidies provided to make corn-based alternative sources of energy has been an expensive failure, for the government and the public. Corn-based ethanol greatly inflates the price of corn whether for corn flakes, food for cattle and pigs (and therefore meat products all go up in price), and even corn-based syrups and sweeteners (that makes soft drinks and snacks go up in price).

As New York Mayor Bloomberg has made clear, sugar is a killer. It is bad for humans to consume, even worse for your health than smoking. All of the hidden sugar in the American diet leads to obesity, diabetes, "diabesity," and even Alzheimer's and Dementia are being referred to by doctors as Type III Diabetes. Thirty years ago – none of the fifty states had an obesity problem. Now, all fifty states have obesity healthcare cases in epidemic proportions. There are no less than two dozen films available on Netflix streaming that show the problems of sugar in the American diet. It seems that PBS public television has a special every Sunday by some notable doctor talking about how deadly sugar in the American diet is to the average American. Both the <u>New York Times Magazine</u> and <u>60 Minutes</u> have had cover stories on the dangers of sugar. We are literally killing our children as well as ourselves. But that is for another book, another day.

The **incredible**, fantastic, unbelievably "good" sugar is **inedible** sugar, that we can get from Mexico at two cents a pound or from our new free-trade partner Colombia at one cent a pound. But even at two cents a pound, that would be $40 per ton of inedible sugar. Each ton of inedible sugar at $40 per ton could produce 140 gallons of sugar-based ethanol. It would take more than **three** barrels of oil at $100 per barrel for West Texas Intermediate or at $120 per barrel for Brent Crude to produce the same amount of energy.

There is no question that you would not use sugar-based ethanol in a high performance, high octane car like a Maserati, but how many average Americans have a Maserati? Instead, most ordinary automobiles manufactured after 1990 can be retro-fitted with a device that costs about $120 and you just need a friendly teenager/gearhead or a local service station to install the device for you, and it will allow your car to accept sugar-based fuel as well as regular gasoline.

In most states, you can build an in-house "still" for yourself to distill spirits and get a permit for free, as long as you are not selling drinkable alcohol and you are making less than 50 gallons a day. Obviously, the sugar-based fuel is for your car and is not fit for human consumption. You should, and we do, put a "skull and crossbones" on the container, and keep it away from children. Do not store it; just put it in your gas tank.

If you Google "making your own still" or "creating sugar-based ethanol," you will find several offers for directions on how to make your own still for between $39 and $79. Many people who make in-home wine or beer already understand that just by adding sugar to water plus some yeast will create the alcoholic mash. You then take that mash to begin the distilling process, which just evaporates the "water" from the "alcohol" mix to produce the 90% pure alcohol. If there is one industry that goes back to the beginning days of the Republic, it is how to make "moonshine" or "white-lightning" or "bathtub" gin. Whatever your poison of preference, Americans have been making alcohol, liquor, and booze longer and better than anyone including the French and Italians. Remember, wine poured in your car will just ruin the engine, but authentic and pure Kentucky or Tennessee "moonshine" can power it.

Even our first President, George Washington, had five stills on his Virginia farm that produced 11,000-15,000 gallons of alcohol per year. Even to this day, most states will give a person a permit for free to have his own homemade still, as long as the alcohol will not be sold or distributed; and as we stated, our brand of ethanol is to be put in your car, not in your mouth.

Last year, the typical American spent over $4,200 a year on gas. Figure 1,100 gallons a year at $3.50-$3.80 per gallon, the highest annual cost in American history. That means it takes 20-25 gallons of gas to fill up the typical American car on Saturday or Sunday for the coming week, and that means $80-$100 per fill up. With sugar-based fuel, the person could distill the same 20 gallons at a cost of

40 cents per gallon and fill up the family car for eight to ten dollars a week from the family's homemade George Washington-type still.

Why is this important? Because Brazil as a nation is already energy independent and sees no reason to send troops to Iraq or Iran to keep open the Straits of Hormuz. Brazil has an embarrassment of natural riches and can produce enough sugar-based ethanol to fuel its cars so that it can export sugar, tobacco, and oil to China to keep the Dragon well-fed and happy. Brazil spends no money to "police" the World and is actually hiring more American engineers than America is at the present time because of all of the energy projects, infrastructure, and building projects going on there. Strangely enough, Brazil has purposefully increased the cost of its sugar-based fuels to prop up its budding oil industry. Brazil has other natural resources like hydro-electric power and advanced technologies from prominent American companies like General Electric, whose reported growth in Brazil has been dramatic, if not positively phenomenal; where its growth in America has been stagnant or even non-existent.

Brazil is without a doubt a natural resources superpower; but so are we. A little-known American Government report actually states that America could grow more sugar cane more profitably than Brazil. If we add our free trade agreements with Mexico and Colombia, we can produce more sugar-based fuel than Brazil, even cheaper than Brazil can. Also, assume that the Castro brothers die or are replaced in the next decade, and Cuba can once again become a sugar producing colony for America.

Imagine oil tankers crossing the Gulf of Mexico filled with tons of sugar instead of barrels of oil. No Somalian pirates, no terrorist attacks, no threats to close the Straits of Hormuz or threats by OPEC to raise prices. Imagine a **renewable** energy source that is abundant, cheap, clean-burning, environment-friendly and American – whether from North America or Latin America, it is still ours or in friendly hands.

But what about refining? Since the Environmental Protection Agency (EPA) was founded in the early 1970's, it has not approved a single new refinery as being clean enough and the cost to improve and update old refineries has caused many refineries to be shut down or go out of business. Entities not involved in the oil refining business – such as Delta Airlines – have been forced to buy refineries to insure a future source of jet fuel if more refineries close.

Now imagine large, clean distilleries set up in Louisiana to replace old, dirty refineries. The EPA would not oppose a new

"Grey Goose" premium vodka distillery on the Bayou, whereas a new oil refinery would be dead on arrival. Even Alaska has had problems getting permission to build a refinery in Valdez at the end of the Alaskan pipeline. Currently, there is a 60 Million gallon a year ethanol distillery for sale in Louisiana for less than $5,000,000. So, we could buy 100 active distilleries across the country for one failed Solyndra? How many jobs would that create? And add "sugar-fuel" distribution to the Wal-Mart in your town or the five liquor stores in your town – buy a case of sugar-based fuel at your local store for $5.00 to $6.00 and that will get you through the week.

There are already small machine-based sugar distilleries available for $10,000 a piece, but a personal still can be put together at a cost of $200 to $500 even with brand new parts. Junk-yard distillers can be put together by creative people at almost no cost at all. The device to make your car sugar-friendly costs a one-time $120 fee and perhaps $50 for an instruction manual or the labor to have someone install it.

Therefore, imagine a small business, the sort that the IRS-CID under the President has raided not once but twice. The same small business that has been hit with over $5,000,000 in nonsensical tax penalties under Code Section 6708 that no one from the President to the Commissioner of the IRS or anyone from the GAO or the Department of Justice even understands. The type of penalties that the National Taxpayer Advocate has referred to as "unconscionable if not unconstitutional." Yes, that small business, just like the one you own or that you or your parents worked for at one time.

Still imagining. Now why bring that sore subject up in this chapter? Because the President authorized and supported a $500,000,000 government loan for a crony of his that was a campaign bundler for the President's campaign (a "legal" version, supposedly, of what Andrew Young did for John Edwards that the Justice Department spent Millions of taxpayer dollars on for a pointless trial to criminalize bad behavior). But what was allegedly illegal for John Edwards to do, was just fine for the President's cronies to do, and they were rewarded with a $500,000,000 loan to build Solyndra. The President even bragged about Solyndra on television. The Department of Justice has spent Billions of dollars in prosecuting similar non-crimes for the IRS-CID for tax penalties that should never have been on the books. IRS tax penalties are strangling small businesses, and to enforce these devastating penalties costs the American taxpayers Billions of dollars on wasted salaries at the IRS, the IRS-CID, the Justice Department and the Department of Labor. Government raids on small businesses in

America cost over a Billion dollars just last year alone.

The President says he is "clueless" as to what can be done to bring down the price of energy in the United States. As he has said, "There is no silver bullet." Well, Mr. President, let us try this: Instead of funding your campaign buddy's science project at Solyndra, [and you **let him get his money out first**, and stiffed the American taxpayers (just between us, Mr. President – if John Edwards or I had done that – well, I probably would have been indicted already, not to mention having my office raided for a third time, but that is beside the point) leaving the taxpayers to pick up the entire $500,000,000 boondoggle for Solyndra], let's give all the small businesses in America making more than $250,000 a year a special tax deduction of $1,000 to build a company still to provide sugar fuel for their employees' fuel needs. There are 750,000 small businesses in America that make more than $250,000 a year. How do we know that? Because there are 25,000,000 small businesses but only 3% will benefit from the Bush (43) tax cuts or be hurt by the President's cancellation of the Bush (43) tax cuts. The three percent of 25,000,000 small businesses equals 750,000 small businesses that all the fighting is about between the two parties. Assuming 15 employees per business, and 1,000 gallons per year per employee for family fuel costs, that would be 15,000 gallons of sugar-based fuel per year from the small company still. Well, George Washington had family-farm stills that produced 15,000 gallons of alcohol per year in 1750, even before America was a nation. Remember the Whiskey Rebellion of 1791-1794?

If each small business of 15 employees in America puts together the same type of family-farm still that George Washington did for his family at a cost of $500 and purchased 15 ethanol converters for each employee's car at $120 a piece for $1,800, for a total of under $2,500 for the company independent fuel project. Giving each of the qualifying 750,000 businesses a **WHISKIE** (Washington Home Individual Small-business Key Initiative for Energy-independence) tax deduction of $2,000 would cost the Government approximately $600 per company in a 30% tax bracket, or roughly $450,000,000 for the entire nation to be energy independent. That is $50,000,000 less than the President spent on Solyndra and his cash-bundling political cronies; and now we have made 750,000 small businesses and over 20,000,000 American families energy independent from the Middle East.

Now, do we really think 750,000 small businesses are going to set up stills like George Washington did? No, of course not, but that is not the point. And there is no reason to complicate the Tax Code with one more tax deduction or tax credit, no matter how well intentioned it may be. The point is that the technology is already available to make America energy independent, and it has been available to Americans to have a still on their family farm or in the back of the garage or the office building, just like George Washington did 260 years ago. Energy costs for a small business' employees could go from $60,000-$80,000 per year down to a few thousand per year for the whole company and their families. The water is plentiful and free and even recycled or dirty water can be used for this project because no one is drinking the fuel and the water will be evaporated during the distillation process.

We do not need tax credits or tax deductions or federal loans for the President's cronies – we just need common sense and to get the EPA, ATF and other Washington bureaucratic administrators of liquor off our backs. Allow free and ample permits for up to 15,000 gallons per year for non-drinkable alcohol, instead of sending ATF people into forests to look for marijuana plants or giving automatic weapons to Mexican drug lords.

Once every American individual and every small business **can be** energy independent, someone will become the local "distiller" of choice for the neighborhood. The best of those neighborhood distillers will become the distiller for the town; and the best of those will become the best in the county, the state and then the region. Then there will be a new John D. Rockefeller or Sam Walton of distilled energy who makes cheap fuel available to everyone across the country, wherever they may be.

The President and his Solyndra-crony friends are part of the problem; they are not part of any solution. When the President says that he has "no solution or silver bullet" for the energy problems facing our nation, you should take his word for it, believe him, and then vote for someone who will at least explore the possible solutions out there, even if they are not perfect. Allowing small businesses to set up a still to produce and provide sugar-based fuel for their employees would be a good start in the right direction. If we invest in anything as a nation, it should be in cost-effective energy solutions, delivery of those solutions, and the infrastructure to support them.

CHAPTER EIGHT
HOW HEALTHCARE CAN BE FREE

Many political pundits have expressed the same cynical thought: "If you think healthcare is expensive now, wait until it is free."

The truth is that they confuse pure "healthcare," the cost of which has gone down dramatically over the years – think for example of Wal-Mart prescription drugs for $4.00 per prescription for 30 days for generic drugs that once cost $70-$100 per month as brand name drugs – with "health insurance" that has consistently gone up 12-15% per year, and will go up 40-60% if the President's "affordable" healthcare plan goes into effect. Health insurance for the American family has gone up 120% over the past ten years. Suffice it to say, if the President is re-elected and his plan goes into effect in 2014, America will be bankrupted. The expected cost of the President's plan has gone from $800 Billion to $1.8 Trillion before it has even been implemented. The provisions that everyone likes, such as young people staying on their parents' health policies until Age 26 have already been adopted by the major carriers. The killer provisions and the penalty for the individual mandate do not start until 2014, and by then it is too late.

So, how can we decouple healthcare – which should be a "right" as it is a necessity – with "health insurance" which is more of a luxury and a privilege rather than an "inalienable" right? Remember that Blue Cross and Blue Shield, United Healthcare, CIGNA and Aetna (the BUCA companies) are all relatively recent creations – all being created in the last 30–40 years. The predecessor companies of Aetna and Connecticut General go back many more years, but they were in different businesses then, and even older insurance companies actually left the "health insurance" market during the same time period.

The McCarran Ferguson Act of 1945 guarantees that the regulation of all insurance issues will be left to the States. The Tenth Amendment of the Constitution reserves to the States and the People anything not mentioned in the Constitution. The Eleventh Amendment of the Constitution guarantees the sovereignty of the States.

All of these Constitutional niceties are irrelevant of course; if the President wants to make sure everyone has "health insurance." There is no question that the "individual mandate" is unconstitutional as a penalty, and even as a "tax" the Supreme Court questions the wisdom of the President's mandatory health insurance program. However, the next President need only grant an **exemption** to all of the States and all of the businesses, just as Speaker Nancy Pelosi has done for various businesses in the San Francisco area.

But is "health insurance" the problem, or is making "health-care" available to all Americans at no cost the true goal? And how is that even possible? Is there a solution that makes access to basic healthcare available to all at affordable rates (i.e. "free"), and if we provide insurance to Federal workers and Congressmen at no cost to them, why not make a Federal insurance program available to all without the "unconstitutional" individual mandate?

Additionally, every American could be signed up for a free HMO in their neighborhood. The Government could get out of the insurance business by staffing free clinics with doctors and nurses that received full scholarships to attend medical school or receive a nursing degree, similar to how ROTC provides college scholarships in exchange for four years of military service. VA hospitals could be converted into centers of excellence to attract the best and brightest doctors, with care provided free to the public as well as veterans. If we pay for "free healthcare" in Iraq and Afghanistan, why not in Indiana and Alabama as well?

Finally, community medical clinics could be established every-where that are paid for by local businesses, public charity, and government grants. Healthcare alliances could be established that would take care of minor medical problems and issue prescriptions. Prescription drug cards could be issued to everyone that was a member of the HMO or the healthcare alliance for free.

This would solve the healthcare issues for 95% of all Americans at little or no cost to the government. There is no need to put the government in the "insurance" business, when most Americans just need a doctor to talk to, run some tests, and then issue a prescription. Save the hospitals and the emergency rooms for truly catastrophic accidents and ailments.

CHAPTER NINE

THE PETTIBONE PARADOX

The Pettibone Tavern is a famous Revolutionary War landmark in Connecticut, not far from the famous Connecticut Charter Oak Tree where the Connecticut Charter was hidden. The Pettibone Tavern is named for Colonel Pettibone's son, Captain Pettibone, who died on Christmas Day in 1776 during Washington's famous crossing of the Delaware just prior to the Battle of Trenton. Captain Pettibone, as an officer, had read to his troops that day Thomas Paine's famous classic *"The American Crisis"* which begins with the immortal words:

These are the times that try men's souls. The summer soldier and the sunshine patriot will, in this crisis, shrink from the service of their country; but he that stands it now, deserves the love and thanks of man and woman. Tyranny, like hell, is not easily conquered; yet we have this consolation with us, that the harder the conflict, the more glorious the triumph. What we obtain too cheap, we esteem too lightly: it is dearness only that gives every thing its value. Heaven knows how to put a proper price upon its goods; and it would be strange indeed if so celestial an article as FREEDOM should not be highly rated. Britain, with an army to enforce her tyranny, has declared that she has a right (not only to TAX) but "to BIND us in ALL CASES WHATSOEVER," and if being bound in that manner, is not slavery, then is there not such a thing as slavery upon earth. Even the expression is impious; for so unlimited a power can belong only to God.

The Pettibone Tavern is also famous for the meeting that led to Captain Noah Phelps and Captain Pettibone helping Ethan Allen and others from Connecticut and Massachusetts to seize the cannons of Fort Ticonderoga in 1775 and get them to Boston to beat the British blockade. Captain Phelps and Captain Pettibone also helped get some of the cannons down to General Washington for the battles in Trenton and Princeton. Though Captain Pettibone died Christmas Day in Washington's attack on the British in Trenton, Captain Phelps went on to become General Phelps and was one of Connecticut's members to the Constitutional Convention of 1787. Most importantly, Noah Phelps' mother was Abigail Pettibone – the name of the ghost that is said to haunt the Tavern to this very day.

Steeped in Revolutionary War history, the Pettibone Tavern was also famous for instituting the first combination of an HRA – Health Reimbursement Account with the brand new HSA – Health Savings Account. (Established January 1, 2003) One small event in American benefits history, and one big step for the Pettibone Tavern's employees that never had health insurance in the past. But there was one problem: the employees all thought the program was "too expensive," and no one wanted to sign up.

The program was a High Deductible Plan that required the employee to contribute $1,500 over the year and the Employer would match that $1,500 for each employee. If the employee's medical claims were over $3,000, then the insurance carrier paid 100% of the claims. The employee's weekly cost was about $30, which could be taken out of his or her paycheck. If an employee had no claims, the $1,500 would build up tax-free in the HSA reserve account until it is needed in the future to pay medical bills.

Despite the low cost and wonderful benefits, no one wanted to join the plan. When asked why, virtually all of the young people felt that they were healthy and invincible and they would rather spend the $30 per week drinking with friends. Older people in management knew how irresponsible this was, but this is the same reaction the President will face when he tries to get young people to sign up for the health insurance that they do not feel they need and is too expensive. Clearly it is a lifestyle choice. Auto insurance is only mandatory if you want to drive. No car? No auto insurance. But health insurance is really a misnomer – it is actually "sickness" insurance, and if you are young and healthy, then clearly you can go without.

Finally, after getting the cost down to $17 per week, some of the employees were interested, but clearly not the majority necessary to get guaranteed issue (everyone accepted without evidence of insurability). When the "holdouts" were asked what they wanted or needed – the answer was an incredible surprise: all of the young people wanted the insurance for free and did not care about the savings element of the HSA. In effect, they wanted the Employer to pay the cost of the insurance and self-fund the employee's half of the $3,000 deductible. Their thought process was that if they hit the proverbial telephone pole or were taken to the hospital in an ambulance, they would be glad that they had the insurance coverage. As for the $1,500 deductible; they could beg, borrow, or steal that money from their parents – or someone – to pay their share of the deductibles and the co-pays on the insurance program. If they went through the year with just a couple of doctor visits, they could handle the $20 co-pay on the visits and the $10 co-pay on the prescription drugs. If they were not sick at all, as they thought would be the case, they would not be wasting their precious "beer" money on health insurance.

The President will see the "Pettibone Paradox" first hand all across America as, one by one, America's young people will gamble with their health. There were, of course, several terrible accidents that were all taken care of by the Pettibone health insurance plan, but more importantly, one of the women managers had a very serious medical problem that usually only women have, and her bill came to a whopping $48,000; and that was after all of the insurance carrier repricing and discounts. Her part of the bill was only $1,500 which she happily paid herself, relieved that she would not be one of the Millions of Americans that are forced to declare bankruptcy every year. The problem that the President will find in 2014 in instituting any type of mandatory health insurance purchase mandate is that both the Employer and the employee will each have incentive not to participate. The Employer will rather pay the $2,000 penalty than pay $12,000 a year or more for health insurance under the new law. The Employer secretly hopes that the employees will all go with some new Government-sponsored insurance exchange. The employee on the other hand will pay the penalty or the tax rather than buying insurance because of the Pettibone Paradox, and because health insurance premiums will skyrocket when everyone with chronic health problems must be taken by the carriers. The truth is that the President's health insurance plan is misguided and is just a regulatory bonanza for the health insurance company monopolies that exist across the country (many states have only one or two of the major BUCA monsters available to them, i.e. the

Blue Cross Companies, United Healthcare, CIGNA and Aetna). For the first time in history, the American people will be ordered by the Government to buy a product. And the President wants 16,000 IRS Special Agents to supervise and patrol the American people and penalize those who do not sign up. If you think the EPA is bad for energy and the economy, and the FAA is bad for air travel, just wait until you experience healthcare under the watchful eyes of the IRS-CID (Criminal Investigation Division).

The truth is that the President is wrong and has confused providing healthcare with health insurance. The young people have it right, and they want the Government to provide them with "free" healthcare and "free" catastrophic insurance, and let them beg, borrow, or steal the $1,500 or $2,500 they need to pay their fair share – after they get sick or have an accident. In fact, the young people are right and the numbers will tell the story after the President's plan is implemented in 2014. Healthcare costs and the cost of health insurance are running at three times the cost of inflation. More and more Employers are either abandoning their health insurance programs or shifting more and more of the cost to their employees. But there is a better way. Studies have shown the following to be the real costs of healthcare:

- 80% of Employees cost less than $800/year on healthcare expenses;

- The next 10% spend less than $1,250/year on healthcare;

- Only 5% of the Employee population comprises over 50% of the typical Employee's healthcare expenses.

Healthcare costs are rising dramatically and the cost of health insurance is rising even faster. The average cost of health insurance in the United States is:

- 2010 - $428.00 per month for SINGLE Employee only; $5,130.00 per year for SINGLE Employee coverage;

- 2010 - $1,177.00 per month for FAMILY coverage; or $14,125.00 per year for FAMILY coverage;

- 2011 - the cost was $9,821.00 for the average Employee per year.

What was the money spent on? Nearly 96% of all employee patient claims are for doctor visits. These visits include fees for X-rays, laboratory costs, unexpected trips to the Emergency Room, having outpatient surgery or just run-of-the mill prescription drugs. So it is true: very few people have large, catastrophic claims.

In fact, only about 6% of the people will have claims over $5,000. That means that the traditional fully insured program is a waste of money for 94% of the employee population. The problem is that we do not know who will be sick next year and who will have a large claim in the future. We do not know who will be in the unlucky 6% that account for the bulk of the Employer's claims. Therefore, the typical Employer wastes as much as 80% – 90% of the employee's insurance expense by buying a full health insurance policy for 100% of their employees when only 5% – 6% of the employees really need catastrophic coverage or full healthcare coverage above $5,000.

Virtually all of the employees at a typical company could be covered with a prescription drug card and a health insurance plan that pays a maximum benefit of $10,000 per year. The young people will tell you that the company – or the Government – should pick up the cost of health insurance with a $5,000 deductible, and they will find some way to pay that $5,000 shortfall after they get out of the hospital (beg, borrow, or steal), but no one will need to declare bankruptcy to pay healthcare bills. The following chart bears witness to the Pettibone Paradox, and gives testament to the fact that the young people are right, and the President is wrong.

BASIC HEALTHCARE INDUSTRY FACTS

Money Spent On Medical Care	Percentage Of	Aggregate % Of	Per 1,000 Employees
No Medical Expenses - $0	33%	33%	330
$1 – $500	40%	73%	400
$501 –$1,000	9%	82%	90
$1,000 – $2,000	7%	89%	70
$2,001 – $5,000	6%	95%	60
$5,001 – $10,000	3%	98%	30
$10,001 – 25,000	1.2%	99.2%	12
$25,001 – $50,000	.5%		5
$50,001 – $100,000	.2%	99.9%	2
$100,001 – And Up	.1%		1

How much would a $5,000 deductible plan cost to cover everyone – with a prescription drug card and full access to any hospital or doctor in their network? The chart shows that the President's plan of enforced health insurance would be a **waste of money** for most Americans. It would bankrupt America and make the health insurance companies rich. A better approach would allow welfare benefit plans to cover the first $5,000 and the Government covers catastrophic claims above $100,000 – a program that can be done at $100 per month for every uninsured American.

THE
AMERWRECKERS

CHAPTER TEN
WAKE UP AMERICA!

WAKE UP...WAKE UP...WAKE UP! The IRS-CID is outside your door. You are away on business. Your wife, who is also a mother of six, is home alone with your youngest daughter, getting her ready for school. Without warning, two dozen of the President's "Special Agents" of the IRS-CID break into your house surprising your wife and daughter. Almost all of the IRS Special Agents are large men, heavily armed, with bulletproof vests on. There has been no warning. There has been no Notice of Deficiency, no Information Document Request, no notice of any audit, no audit summons, or any letters from the IRS questioning any tax return that you or your family has ever filed. This true story was covered by most newspapers around the Country between April 13 and 16, 2010 (for example, see **Boston.com** for just one of the many stories; just search for Fort Wayne, Indiana IRS raid).

This is no mere violation of the Fourth Amendment of the Constitution of the United States. This is an armed commando raid on ordinary Americans – on United States citizens. The President was upset that a Boston police officer wrongfully arrested a Harvard professor who happened to be an African-American, and that "misunderstanding" led to beers in the Rose Garden of the White House. The Attorney General has written a speech called

"A Nation of Cowards" regarding race, but how does the Attorney General not investigate Special Agents of the IRS that work for him that have violated the fundamental laws of this Country and the Constitution itself?

This book is written for you in the hope that it is not too late to save the Country from the road that it is currently on. You must vote Republican in these upcoming Congressional and Senate elections because if you don't, you just may become a victim of the President's new IRS-CID "wealth-squad" attacks, even if you are not wealthy. No warning – only a sealed search warrant based on lies or innuendo from your neighbors or business competitors or corrupt informants – a sealed warrant that will take you months or years to unseal. Don't think that it can happen to you? It happened to Senator Ted Stevens, the longest serving Republican Senator in the United States Senate. If the Government can raid a Senator's house without probable cause, how can you possibly be safe? The Attorney General was so shocked by the egregious prosecutorial misconduct against Senator Stevens that he made a motion to have all charges against him dropped. But the misconduct by the Government destroyed Senator Stevens' reputation, career and also his life. Senator Stevens, a great American, died of a broken heart in disgrace, with no chance to clear his name.

You are probably not a Senator though, and neither is your wife. You are a hard-working businessman that has applied for financial aid for your college-bound children. Your wife is a homemaker and mother of six, and you live in a middle class neighborhood in Fort Wayne, Indiana. You do not live in Beverly Hills or in a New York City penthouse – there is absolutely nothing about your lifestyle that would lead anyone to believe you are fudging on your taxes or living beyond your means. But, even if you were cheating on your taxes, why did you not receive an audit notice? What was the reason for the armed commando raid on an innocent housewife and her daughter?

Armed commando raids like this were meant to be stopped by the Roth Hearings, the Webster Commission Task Force, and the passage of the IRS Restructuring and Reform Act of 1998. Attending the Roth Hearings on IRS abuse of the American Taxpayer, deceased New York Democratic Senator Daniel Moynihan was heard to say, *"My God, we must stop these armed commando raids on American citizens."*

Congress did pass the necessary legislation to protect American citizens, and the Webster Commission Task Force was established to review whether the IRS-CID commandos were following the rules that the IRS had imposed on them. When the Government was sued years later in one particular Bivens Action, the IRS-CID agents testified that they could not even remember what the alleged "probable cause" was that required the armed commando raid in the first place; rather than serving an administrative audit summons, subpoena, or even a search warrant in the "least intrusive means possible." (See IRS Manual – yes, the IRS's own rule book – Part 9.4.6.1). (A "Bivens Action" is named after and refers to a Supreme Court case, *Bivens v. Six Unknown Federal Agents*, 403 U.S. 388 (1971), which allows for a civil tort claim against the Government and/or Government officials for violations of the Constitutional rights of citizens during one of these raids).

Do you expect the Courts to help save you? Forget about it. In all of those thousand page bills that Congress passed without reading, they put in provisions that allow the IRS to assess $200,000 penalties that can grow to over a Million Dollars. These penalties are not subject to any judicial review and can be imposed by any out-of-control Field Agent of the IRS. See the Chapter "The Section 6708 Affair."

But if you want to sue the Government, it is a very difficult thing to do. This is true even though the Supreme Court has taken away "qualified immunity" from the IRS commandos who do not follow the rules (see the IRS Manual Part 9). But in several hundred "Bivens-type Actions" brought against the IRS commandos to date, none were successful because the Courts always felt the "IRS must be right" or would say "I just cannot bring myself to find bad faith on the part of the Government."

As if that is not bad enough, once the innocent victims bring an action against the Government, the Government in turn then brings an action against them, tells the jury that this person committed tax fraud, and a totally innocent person spends four years in jail. If you don't believe it, see the case of Dr. Daniel Levito in which even Judge – now Supreme Court Justice – Alito states that Dr. Levito was clearly a victim of a violation of the Fourth Amendment during a commando raid of his small veterinary clinic where the Agents sent away clients of the firm, sent the employees home, and ransacked his clinic. Because Dr. Levito had the gall to sue the Government, years later he would be indicted for tax evasion and his wife was given probation for testifying against her own husband because he was exercising his First Amendment rights in advocating a book on tax avoidance. It seems only fair – since the Government put him out of business as a veterinarian – that Dr. Levito became an anti-Government, anti-tax advocate. Some of the arguments that

Dr. Levito and his partners make in "their" book are totally frivolous and the IRS now has a portion of their website dedicated to these "frivolous", if not borderline illegal tax evasion ideas. Those types of "frivolous" or "illegal" tax evasion arguments are nowhere to be found in this Book. In fact, every single tax saving idea mentioned in this Book can find support in the IRS's own Revenue Rulings, Regulations, Tax Court cases, and the IRS's own website.

The protections for the American Taxpayer are also found on the IRS's own website and in the IRS's own Manual, which is available online. The Webster Commission Report is available in PDF format online. Remember, William Webster was a former Judge and the head of the CIA, and even he was shocked by the level of Government abuse of innocent American taxpayers by the IRS-CID.

The reason for writing this Book is that we are genuinely frightened that the President wants to hire 16,000 new Special Agents who will engage in **Sealed** Search Warrant, secret, armed commando raids on innocent American citizens and businesses. We use the word "innocent" because in 90% of the armed commando raids, there is **no** later assessment of taxes. After a two year investigation following the raids that disrupted the business, there is no "crime" or even tax deficiency found that would have warranted the raid in the first place. Remember, this is the IRS-CID, not the FBI or Drug Enforcement Agency or Bureau of Alcohol, Tobacco & Firearms. So, instead of serving an audit summons or subpoena, they have several dozen armed commandos in Kevlar vests with IRS-CID printed on the front, executing a **sealed** search warrant that you will not see for several months to several years after you file a Rule 41(g) motion in order to get your property back and unseal the warrant and affidavit.

Did we mention the President wants to hire 16,000 new Special Agents for the IRS-CID just to do this sort of work? The Government will only hire 800 new SEC Agents to keep Wall Street in line. This, even after the Bernie Madoff debacle and Goldman Sachs paying a fine of only a half-Billion dollars for helping to bring down the economies of the Western World with toxic mortgages. Notice that friends of Goldman convinced the Government to put in $200 Billion to save AIG with $60 Billion going directly to the coffers of Goldman Sachs from the AIG guarantee of bad mortgage bonds. Lehman Brothers was allowed to go under, while AIG was saved by the Government so it could make good on the guarantees that Goldman Sachs had hoped to exploit in creating the toxic subprime mortgage market in the first place. Goldman has not had to plead guilty to anything or even admit fault. The $550 Million fine is two weeks of revenue for Goldman – a mere traffic ticket – relatively speaking. But the same Government that will fine doctors and other small businesses up to $800,000 for failing to report a "listed" or "reportable" transaction that they did not even know they had participated in, and this is four to five years after the small business had adopted an ordinary pension plan with life insurance in it, lets big Wall Street firms off the hook so that they can pay record bonuses to their executives two years in a row after allegedly the greatest financial crisis since the Depression. Of course, you cannot believe it, because you think this is America, and excessive penalties like that would violate the "excessive fines" clause of the Eighth Amendment, the "takings" clause of the Fifth Amendment, and even the *"ex post facto"* clause of the Constitution, because fines of this magnitude are clearly "punishments" and not traffic fines or ordinary civil penalties. But these "punishments" are meted out every day to small, unsuspecting businesses that do not have thousand-dollar-an-hour tax attorneys to defend them as does Wall Street.

The America that you grew up in is rapidly vanishing and being subsumed by an overly-intrusive Government whose uncontrolled spending is threatening your family's future financial prosperity, freedom, and in certain cases – your life. The $15 Trillion current deficit and $70 Trillion in unfunded future liabilities will either be handled by bankrupting America now or from the tears and loss of freedom by your children and grandchildren. The deficit will not go away by itself and the President has signaled that he will hire 16,000 new IRS-CID Special Agents who will break the law with armed commando raids into the homes and businesses of innocent American citizens. Nothing like this has happened in this Country since British troops would routinely break into the homes of Boston housewives while their husbands were at work in order to demand money to pay for an out of touch, out of control, and overly intrusive Government in England. Make no mistake: no one in Washington cares about you. If they would raid a United States Senator's home, indict him on totally bogus charges, and find him guilty through egregious prosecutorial misconduct, then you have no hope of being safe. Instead of passing the Dodd-Frank banking reform bill, Congress could have instead reinstated the Glass-Steagall Act, which served us well for 70 years. The same is true with the "up-tick rule" to stop the relentless shorting of stock by greedy and well-connected Hedge Funds, almost all of whom have accounts or friends at Goldman Sachs.

You, unfortunately, probably do not have a clue as to what we are talking about, or how this will negatively affect your future, because no one from the Government has pointed out to you all of the terrible things hidden in all of these thousand page legislative acts that no one reads. Even at this late date, you ask your candidate for the Presidency, the Senate or Congress how they feel about abortion, the death penalty, gay marriage, or gun control issues (issues which members of Congress could not possibly control even if they wanted to). Washington is squandering your resources and the Nation's resources at an unprecedented rate. You must vote Republican in this election so America can return to its greatest years of 1994-2000 when we had an intelligent progressive President in the White House with a Republican Congress filled with deficit-hawks that did not care what anyone did behind closed doors.

Rest assured, if you do not vote Republican in 2012, your doors will eventually be kicked down by an out of control IRS-CID Special Agent that must find more and more tax revenue through fear and intimidation just to **pay the interest** on our national debt. Forget the principal or future entitlement programs, just the interest on our National debt will take up our entire tax revenue when interest rates hit 6-7%. The Government is out of control and is dangerously close to being willing to sacrifice the future liberty and prosperity of its citizens on an altar of ever-growing deficits to fund an overly intrusive and invasive Government.

To find an example of what America will be like with another 16,000 Special Agents hired to invade innocent American businesses and homes, one need look no further than Special Agent Shaun Schrader, who has no problem providing false information to a magistrate judge in order to get a **sealed** search warrant approved so that the armed commandos of the IRS-CID can raid an innocent business without giving them any warning. Special Agent Schrader is, in fact, famous for raiding popular restaurants at lunch hour, during their busiest time of day to make sure that you, patrons and proprietors alike, fear the power of the IRS. One restaurant he raided in Rochester, Minnesota was run by a local chef who had worked his way up from nothing to being one of the best known chefs in the state. Special Agent Schrader operates out of the Milwaukee IRS office, but he is known to travel all over the Country to tell lies about small businesses in order mislead the local magistrate judge into signing a **sealed** search warrant, so that the business will have no idea what is about to befall them. Special Agent Schrader never follows the rules that are clearly outlined in Part 9 of the IRS's own Manual. See, e.g., IRS Manual Part 9.4.6 requiring the IRS to use the least **intrusive method** possible. Special Agent Schrader is exactly the sort of new irresponsible IRS-CID cowboy that you need to fear. He will tell any lie and state any misinformation to support his required affidavit to establish "probable cause" that there is some reason the unsuspecting business – the restaurant in this case – will destroy the evidence that the IRS needs to make their case against them.

Now let us assume, just for the sake of discussion, that this well-known restaurant in Minnesota really was keeping two sets of books. Is an armed commando raid with three or four dozen armed agents with bulletproof vests at **lunch time** really the "least intrusive" way to get that information? How about a raid at eight o'clock in the morning as the IRS-CID did in Fort Wayne to an unsuspecting wife and child? Or how about on a Saturday morning at ten o'clock, when no one ever goes to a restaurant? No: Special Agent Schrader wanted everyone in Minnesota to know this restaurant entrepreneur was suspected of tax fraud.

The only problem with that theory was that they never found the second set of books, or any tax fraud whatsoever. Especially in this day and age, when most people pay their bills at a restaurant with a credit card, wouldn't the "least intrusive manner" as required by the IRS's own Manual be to execute a Third Party Summons on the credit card companies to get all of their payments from that particular restaurant? If the credit card receipts showed $3 Million in gross income for the restaurant and the restaurant only reported $2 Million or $1.5 Million in revenues, then you have a case for tax fraud. What about expenses? The law already says that you must prove each and every deduction. In the future, you will need to report every expenditure over $600 as a small business, even for nondeductible expenditures – which was part of the Healthcare Bill that no Congressman read – and every business in America must justify and document every deduction that it puts on its tax return. Thus, if Special Agent Schrader feels the restaurant is "fudging" or "fiddling" on its taxes, why not issue an audit notice and make the restaurant prove each and every deduction as it is required to do under the tax law? The IRS never did that despite Special Agent Schrader's commando raid, and no tax fraud was ever found against the restaurateur even though his business was raided and his reputation forever tarnished. The family in Fort Wayne was not so lucky, however, and that is one of the reasons why we are writing this Book.

Jim and Denise Simon of Fort Wayne, Indiana received absolutely no warning that they were under investigation by the IRS or the IRS-CID. The agent in charge of the case, Special Agent Paul Muschell, wrote an affidavit to secure the **sealed** search warrant that has been described by professionals to be replete with numerous factual and legal errors, clear misrepresentations of both fact and law. Testimony by Special Agent Muschell appeared to the attorneys involved in the case to be designed to mislead the magistrate judge into granting the search warrant and to have it sealed. In other words, the same sort of affidavit that Special Agent Shaun Schrader might have done, complete with misinformation, misrepresentations, and misleading innuendo just so some magistrate judge would sign the sealed search warrant in violation of the American citizens' Fourth Amendment rights against unreasonable search and seizure.

Neither Jim nor Denise Simon ever had any problems with the IRS in the past, and to this day, there has been no evidence presented that at the time of the illegal raid on the Simon's residence in Fort Wayne, Indiana, that Jim Simon had filed any false or even incorrect tax returns concerning his business affairs. Not only was there no probable cause for the search warrant or to have the search warrant **sealed**, there was absolutely no reason for the raid. Does an armed commando raid of two dozen husky Special Agents with weapons drawn, covered with bulletproof vests, shouting "IRS-CID" at a housewife and her 10-year-old daughter make any sense to you? Please remember that the IRS, in its own Manual, instructs and **requires** the IRS-CID officer in charge to use the **"least intrusive means"** of investigation available in all cases (see IRM Part 9.4.6.7.3.3).

When the storm troopers broke into the house of an American housewife – a mother of six – getting her youngest daughter ready for school, they accused her and her husband (who was overseas on business) with a multitude of crimes including tax evasion, fraud, money laundering, as well as other things that Denise Simon had no comprehension of and clearly did not believe or understand. The reason this is so painfully apparent is that within a few days of the raid, Denise took her own life as she was terrified by what had transpired in her family home. The suicide letters she left behind to each of her six children and her husband are heart-breaking and can be found at www.rememberdenise.org, and at other sites on the Internet.

We will only reprint here the general letter she left behind proclaiming her innocence, as well as her husband's innocence, of any and all crimes of which they were accused:

I am truly innocent of any attempt to evade taxes, launder money, commit fraud or any of the other things I am being accused of. I know of no attempt on Jim's part to willingly or knowingly evade taxes, launder money, commit fraud or any of the other things he is being accused of. However, I also have no faith in the legal system or the ability of the government to seek truth. I am currently a danger to my children. I am bringing armed officers into their home. I am compelled to distance myself from them for their safety. Being innocent is simply not enough for the government.

With my dying breath, I swear Jim & I are innocent.

– Denise Simon

As one might expect, Mr. Simon's attorneys filed all sorts of motions under the Freedom of Information Act (FOIA) to find out what this was all about. His attorneys also filed several motions to unseal the **sealed** search warrant affidavit submitted by Special Agent Muschell. Surprisingly, once the Court unsealed the affidavit, there was no information there to let anyone know what the Simons were actually accused of, what crimes they had allegedly committed, or why some unarmed IRS agent in a suit and a tie could not have served the Simons by mail or even better, sent a Third Party Summons to the banks where the IRS thought the Simons were hiding money. But no, the IRS-CID Special Agent involved felt that the right thing to do was to make material misrepresentations to a magistrate judge so he would sign a **sealed** search warrant that would "legally" allow this armed commando raid on a defenseless American housewife and her youngest daughter. Denise admitted in her suicide notes "that she was terrified of the Government" and "she was not strong enough to fight." Despite protesting her and her husband's innocence, she admitted, "I just don't have any faith in the legal system, and I can't fight this." And she worried that by fighting, "I can only bring danger to my family now."

Where are the beers in the Rose Garden for Jim Simon and Special Agent Paul Muschell? Special Agent Paul Muschell works for the Secretary of the Treasury, who himself was accused of either cheating on his taxes or making some very dumb mistakes for such a very smart guy. Where is the Attorney General's outrage? Unfortunately for both Jim and Denise Simon, they are both white, middle class, hard working Americans, so there is no question that this terrible incident was not motivated by race or sexual orientation, which seem to be the only issues that interest the Justice Department these days – unless they involve marijuana legalization in California or illegal immigration in Arizona. Protection of the American taxpayer's Constitutional rights in Indiana or Minnesota is not even on their radar screen.

Denise Simon is dead and she was killed by Special Agent Paul Muschell, just as if he had actually pulled the trigger. The IRS Restructuring and Reform Act of 1998 and the Webster Commission Task Force of 1999 were meant to end these armed commando raids on unarmed and totally innocent American citizens. The "cowboys" out there like Special Agent Muschell and Special Agent Schrader need to be stopped and brought to justice before their lies to magistrate judges kill someone else. But if the President will not protect you, and the Attorney General and the Department of Justice will not protect you, who can you trust to help you? Well, that brings us full circle as to why you need to vote Republican in this upcoming election. Because the same Congressman and Senator that is **powerless** to help you regulate abortion, the death penalty, gay marriage, or guns and drugs in the streets, is exactly the person who can vote to curtail the monstrous, illegal and unconstitutional activities of the IRS. If you do nothing, the President wants to hire 16,000 more Special Agents like Muschell and Schrader to come after your family or ours. Only Congress can stop that. If you vote to re-elect the President and vote for the Democrat Senator or Congressman this November, you can be sure that your food, energy, and healthcare bills will all be much more expensive, your taxes higher, your freedoms taken away and the future a lot less bright than it could have been – and should have been if we followed the Constitution.

Regardless of who is to blame for the current state of affairs, your future financial security, freedom, and even your life are on the line this time, this election. The wealthy know how to avoid taxes. The big corporations all incorporate offshore companies, and legally pay no taxes. So why do the Special Agents of the IRS-CID pick on people like Denise and Jim Simon? *Because they can.* You do not see Special Agent Schrader planning an IRS-CID raid on Goldman Sachs, do you? Special Agent Muschell and Special Agent Schrader will not be stopped by the President, the Attorney General, the Treasury Secretary or the current Department of Justice. It is only when the IRS is made to account for its actions in front of a new Republican President and a Republican Congress that you will be safe from unauthorized Government intrsions into your affairs and your homes. This Book was written to help you and your family, and we pray that we are not too late.*

---

* Chapter excerpts borrowed with permission from *How Republicans Can Legally Pay No Taxes, Change America, And Save The World.* by Lex Voltaire (Nov. 29, 2010)

CHAPTER ELEVEN
FAST AND SPURIOUS

Roger Clemens was forced to endure a federal trial for a second time accused of "lying to Congress." He was found innocent of all charges after his first trial ended in a mistrial due to egregious prosecutorial misconduct. As there appears to be no crime in Congress lying to America, it begs the question as to why Roger Clemens was put on trial, not just once but twice, and how does the trial of a future Baseball Hall of Fame candidate (who would have been a "shoo-in" if not for these false and scurrilous accusations) benefit the American public? And, with all of the problems facing America, was the enormous amount of money spent on the two trials really a good use of taxpayer dollars? Certainly not.

What was Mr. Clemens actually accused of doing? He adamantly denied using steroids and HGH – the Human Growth Hormone – and he defended his personal honor and stature as of one of the hardest working athletes in the game of baseball. Who said he was lying? An admitted liar, low-life, and bottom feeder was the Government's only witness that claimed Mr. Clemens lied when he stated that he did not use steroids. Why was this an issue for a federal court? If you defame someone on the floor of Congress you cannot be sued. If you defame someone in a court proceeding, it is virtually impossible to be sued. In my own experience, I have seen federal judges put in their opinions that key prosecution witnesses lied – committed perjury on a major issue – and yet the Justice Department did nothing to prosecute these people. So why did the President's Department of Justice go after Roger Clemens?

There is an old political joke that cuts very close to the current reality: How can you tell a Congressman is lying? If his lips move… But seriously, each day the few valuable grains of truth trying to grow in Washington are trampled in the thrashing of the chaff of lies that make up a typical day in Congress. How can lying to Congress be a crime, when lying to America is not?

Who decides who is prosecuted and who is not? The prosecutor in the Justice Department. Who is the boss of the Department of Justice? Attorney General Eric Holder. Now, if Attorney General Holder lies to Congress, who will make the decision to prosecute him? Obviously not Holder's colleagues in the Justice Department, as proven by Holder being the first Attorney General in American history to be held in Contempt of Congress. Does Congressman Darrell Issa have the right to call for his indictment? Just Google "Fast and Furious," the botched ATF gun-running operation where American guns were sold to illegal straw buyers just to show that American guns were being used to kill innocent people in the Mexican Drug Wars. We already knew that, though. There was no reason for "Fast and Furious." Read any of the excellent books on the subject. The Attorney General has denied any prior knowledge of the "Fast and Furious" fiasco. The Attorney General, Eric Holder, has lied to the American people, which is apparently not a crime, but he has also lied to Congress, which is obviously a crime according to Holder's own Justice Department, and stonewalled the investigation into Fast and Furious, which is called obstruction of justice, also a federal crime punishable by five years in jail.

But wait, Eric Holder lied in emails and over the wires of television and radio. Because of his use of the Internet, television, and radio in furtherance of his deceitful scheme to defraud Congress as to his material misrepresentations that he – as Attorney General – knew absolutely nothing about this bogus ATF operation that ended up killing one American border agent and 47,515 North Americans known as Mexicans, Congressman Issa should find the magistrate that will sign the sealed search warrant to seize Eric Holder's computer and emails because the evidence of Eric Holder's wire fraud and lying to Congress is already in print and all over the Internet. Ask Jeff Skilling of Enron notoriety about **honest services fraud** and mail and wire fraud. If we were in England, Eric Holder would already have been forced to resign in disgrace.

The man has no shame and should be indicted for lying to Congress, obstruction of justice, and honest services fraud and wire fraud. Someone in Congress should give Attorney General Holder a taste of his own "search and seizure" and "lying to Congress" medicine.

Instead of being Attorney General, Eric Holder should be facing 20 years in jail. If he were a black man in Boston, he would be indicted already and facing at least 10-20 years like Rodney Gurley (see *US v. Gurley*, No. 10-10310 (D. Mass. May 17, 2012)), that Holder's Department of Justice wants to serve at least 10 years in jail for possession instead of the three years that Judge Young in Boston sentenced him to. If this Justice Department believes in prosecuting Roger Clemens for lying to Congress and John Edwards for lying to his wife, then so, too, must Eric Holder be brought to justice as a "war" criminal. Let me explain just how damaging Eric Holder's "War on Drugs" has been to our neighbor to the South, Mexico. If the President does not fire Eric Holder, and the man does not resign, anyone of Mexican descent voting for the President is condemning their Mexican brothers and sisters to four more years of a terrible war; the most costly war in recent North American history.

Just how terrible are the Mexican Drug Wars? To put things in perspective, let us look at the American wars since World War II and the number of **North American** casualties. Are not Canadian lives and Mexican lives worthy of the same mourning and recognition as American lives? Hopefully, the answer to that question is beyond peradventure or debate.

NORTH AMERICANS KILLED

Gulf War Operation Desert Storm	148
(Including 35 deaths from friendly fire)	
War in Afghanistan	1,984
(Including 157 Canadians)	
Iraq War	3,532

(Including 3,424 since May 1, 2003 when Bush (43)

declared "Mission Accomplished")

War on Terror Since 2001	4,977
Korean War	33,686
Vietnam War	47,424
Mexican Drug Wars	47,515

(Source: Attorney General of Mexico)

(Other Sources say 67,050)

Most of these North Americans were killed by guns manufactured and sold in America. No one I know has died from smoking marijuana, but of all the guns seized by Mexican authorities that were involved in Mexican crimes and Mexican murders, a whopping 87% were from American sources. This is a total failure on the part of the President's Administration. Our "War on Drugs" has not done anything to stop the flow of "party" drugs into this country, but we have supplied most of the weapons that have killed **TEN TIMES** the number of North Americans killed in all of our Wars on Terror, including Afghanistan and Iraq.

The President and his Attorney General have become quite egocentric in claiming credit for successes like killing Osama bin Laden, but are willing to disclaim all responsibility for the botched operation of "Fast and Furious," the War on Drugs (even raiding legal medical marijuana producers in California), and the failed immigration policy of this Administration that has resulted in the **DEPORTATION** of more Mexicans than all other Presidents in U.S. history combined. If you are of Hispanic descent, Latino, Mexican, or whatever, and you vote for the President; then you are not paying attention. The President and Eric Holder are responsible for more ICE raids than at any other time in U.S. History; as well as suing the State of Arizona because it was forced to take action on its own since Washington and the President had no plan to deal with illegal immigration other than to deport innocent, hardworking people, including high school and college valedictorians. If you are proud of your Latino or Hispanic heritage, you cannot possibly vote to re-elect the President and Eric Holder.

Finally, do not forget the case of two border guards – Ignacio Ramos and Jose Compean who were indicted for doing their job as border guards – i.e. stopping drug smugglers – who were sent to prison for shooting a drug smuggler in the buttocks – and later pardoned by Bush (43) after pressure from many circles. The Eric Holder Justice Department has its own disgraceful case that is even worse than the infamous Ramos-Compean Case. Border Guard Jesus Diaz single-handedly took on drug smugglers of a notorious Mexican drug cartel who were smuggling across a large amount of illegal drugs. None of this is in dispute. Agent Diaz was indicted by the same Justice Department that indicted Roger Clemens, and the same U.S. Attorney's Office that indicted Ramos and Compean, but this new U.S. Attorney was appointed by the President and supervised by Eric Holder. Agent Diaz, who was cleared of all wrongdoing by his supervisors at the Border Patrol, was prosecuted by the Eric Holder Justice Department, found guilty, and sentenced to 24 months in jail. What was the alleged crime that warranted a sentence of **TWO YEARS** for a border guard with an impeccable work record? He was allegedly "too rough in putting handcuffs" on one of the armed drug-trafficking cartel members and he allegedly "lied" to a federal investigator during the investigation.

As one of several Congressmen asking for clemency for Agent Diaz, Representative Duncan Hunter petitioned the Attorney General to review the prosecution of Agent Diaz. The response he received from Assistant Attorney General Ronald Weich is an embarrassment to all law-abiding Americans, especially those of Hispanic descent like Agent Diaz. Agent Diaz has done more in the War on Drugs and the Mexican Drug Wars than either Attorney General Holder or Assistant Attorney General Weich. It is a national disgrace that Agent Diaz – a true American hero is in jail, while Eric Holder – a real liar and a real obstructionist of justice is still in office. Instead of **persecuting** Agent Diaz and Roger Clemens, some branch of the Government should be **prosecuting** Eric Holder for his crimes against America, lying to Congress, wire fraud, honest services fraud and his war crimes against the North American citizens of Mexico. Eric Holder is directly responsible for the murder of Border Agent Brian A. Terry and is guilty as an agent-after-the-fact for the cover up of his death by "Fast and Furious" weapons. Eric Holder and his subordinates did everything but pull the trigger of the weapon that killed Agent Terry. If Agent Diaz should be in jail for two years for handcuffing a criminal, then Eric Holder should at least be investigated and prosecuted for his crimes – or at least be investigated by a special prosecutor. Once again – what was Richard Nixon's "crime" that forced him to resign from office?

Just to be clear. If you care about America, if you care about the Border, if you care about Justice and Freedom, and if you care about the Truth, then you cannot, and should not, vote to re-elect the President. Or if you care about Mexico, care about the treatment of immigrants in this country, and the innocent judges, police-men, and border guards being killed in Mexico with American weapons, then you cannot and should not vote for the President, because a vote for the President would be a vote for Eric Holder. The only vote that Eric Holder deserves is a vote of guilty when a jury of his peers tries him for all of his "honest services" crimes against Americans in this country and for his help in killing 47,515 innocent Mexican civilians in the Mexican Drug War which was caused by the Department of Justice in the United States.

At the very worst, Roger Clemens might have lied once to Congress. Eric Holder has repeatedly lied to America and Congress. The Eric Holder led prosecution of Roger Clemens wanted to keep out of the case how despicable the character flaws were of the low-life testifying against him. Just Google it. There was no solid evidence that Roger Clemens lied about anything. Similarly, there was no evidence that Agent Diaz lied to anyone, much less the federal agents questioning him. Agent Diaz was sentenced to two years in jail for doing his job, sto ping drugs coming across the border, and handcuffing a felon. So why is Eric Holder not being investigated and indicted for lying to Congress – obstruction of justice – and for conspiracy in the murder of Agent Terry? Calling Congressman Darrell Issa – what are you waiting for? Demand Eric Holder's resignation and indictment and find a magistrate to seize his computer, cell phone and emails. Just Google "Fast and Furious" and read the books out there on Amazon Kindle. The evidence against Eric Holder is overwhelming. He should be prosecuted for his crimes. Knowing all of this, if you still vote for the President, you also vote for Eric Holder, and you will have Agent Terry's blood on your hands and Agent Diaz's prosecution on your conscience.

CHAPTER TWELVE
BLAME IT ALL ON ELIOT

Eliot Spitzer, like many American politicians, came from a wealthy family and had his father buy him an election to become the Attorney General of the State of New York. There was no doubt that this was a mere stepping stone on his way to becoming Governor of New York and then later President of the United States. Unfortunately, his political career was cut short as he had to resign in disgrace after only a year in office as Governor of the Empire State due to his participation in an elite prostitution and call-girl operation.

Spitzer, as Attorney General, wanted to make a name for himself and was famous for his team of hard nose investigators that brought several actions against alleged Wall Street insiders and market manipulators who, after much trial and tribulation and publicity for Spitzer, were found innocent by a jury or a judge. Spitzer's claim to fame was "bringing down" the Gambino crime family by having them pay $11,000,000 in fines and promise to leave the New York garment industry alone. This is eerily reminiscent of the Government fining Goldman Sachs $500,000,000 (approximately equal to two weeks profits in a good year) for its wrongdoings in the great financial crisis that crippled our country. As history shows, John Gotti did more to control the Gambino family than Eliot Spitzer ever did, and for all of the terrible things that Goldman Sachs did, no one has ever been indicted much less gone to jail.

This is indeed amazing when one considers that "Sir Allen" Stanford received a sentence of 110 years in jail for simply misinvesting and losing seven Billion dollars of client funds. John Corzine misplaced and misinvested two Billion dollars of client funds, but no one has indicted or charged him yet, and Goldman Sachs misappropriated, a.k.a. stole $69-200 Billion Dollars from the American taxpayers' coffers depending on how you do the accounting, and no one has been indicted at Goldman – much less made to pay for their crimes against America. Moreover, no Government Agency has raided John Corzine's home or the offices of Goldman Sachs looking for the misuse of TARP funds, but the Government did raid the offices of Imperial Holdings looking for TARP money misspent on Stranger Originated Life Insurance (STOLI) policies as if lying on a life insurance application was a crime.

The President has been rightfully criticized that his stimulus packages and his rescue packages took money from Main Street taxpayers and funneled it directly to Wall Street bankers. Americans have become poorer – going from an average wealth per household of $126,000 in 2007 to $77,000 in 2011; roughly what the National Household Wealth Average was in 1984. It is bad enough that 2001-2011 was the Lost Decade for investing, but now the average American family has lost nearly **Thirty Years** of national wealth building in four short years; mainly due to high unemployment, low interest rates, decreased wages, and a moribund housing market.

Who is to blame for this national catastrophe? Obviously, the President blames Bush (43), and everyone else blames the President for this national economic debacle. Even President Clinton's most loyal Democratic advisors are calling the President "clueless," in that he ties up and strands rush hour commuters so that he can relentlessly pursue fund raising dinners with movie stars in New York and Los Angeles. Even a casual reader of the daily Wall Street Journal or New York Times could tell the President that there is something wrong with median national household wealth at a total of $77,000 per family and the **average** student loan debt at over $101,000. Here is a "clue" for the President – a truly great stimulus idea: get out of Afghanistan and Pakistan now – and take that Trillion Dollars and pay off every American graduate's student loan. Now graduates would not have to live with Mom and Dad after graduation, and they could afford to go out and buy a home. Once you discovered that Osama bin Laden had been happily living in Pakistan for six years with his four wives, you should have begun the pull out from Afghanistan and Iraq, but you waited for political reasons and wasted yet another Trillion Dollars there.

But if this national malaise is not the President's fault, who can we blame? Once you investigate all of the facts and read all of the books, you will come to the inescapable conclusion that the total collapse of our entire national economy and the evaporation of twenty years of national wealth is the fault of one man's hubris and unbridled political ambition – Eliot Spitzer. Had Eliot Spitzer, as Attorney General, not gone after AIG and Maurice "Hank" Greenberg – the esteemed CEO of AIG – none of these terrible things that have befallen America would have happened. The evidence against Eliot Spitzer is clear, irrefutable, and incontrovertible.

If you grew up as a young insurance executive, Hank Greenberg was your idol, your icon, your Northern Star. Hank Greenberg took over AIG at a young age and transferred a sleepy old line company into an international juggernaut. Insurance is boring. It does not matter if it is Life, Property and Casualty, or Accident and Health. You do not care about insurance until you need it, and if you need it, and do not have it, then it is too late. If you never need it, then you think it is a total waste of time and money; no wonder all the big buildings are owned by insurance companies.

But Hank Greenberg changed all that. Insurance became exciting, and AIG would and could insure any risk, anywhere, and at any time – at a price. While no one was paying attention, AIG and all of its affiliated companies grew internationally and insured any risk you could name. Young people at young companies became rich by insuring nuclear waste dumps or other environmental concerns. Whether insuring the Space Shuttle or an oil tanker, the chances were, the only carrier you could find was an AIG-affiliated company. And everyone knew that Hank Greenberg ran AIG with an iron hand.

Hank Greenberg was the consummate business executive and master of the sleight of hand using off-shore captives to bolster balance sheets and contain risk. A good example of this is the misguided prosecution of the former CEO of General Re, Ronald Ferguson, and the General Counsel of General Re, Elizabeth Monrad, in Connecticut Federal Court. General Re was purchased by Warren Buffett and Berkshire Hathaway, but early in the first financial crisis of October 2000, AIG needed surplus help in bolstering its balance sheets and keeping its coveted AAA rating. Executives at AIG came up with a creative idea, and as executives do in the reinsurance business; they will share that idea with other "go-to" insurance carriers. In the 1990's and early 2000's, there were only two "go-to" carriers: AIG and General Re – which was owned by Berkshire Hathaway.

The idea is very simple, but no American jury will understand it. It is called Finite Reinsurance. One company has a big liability, but it is not sure how large it will be, so it sells the risk to another insurance carrier for a fixed amount of money, and the two companies agree on the terms of the transfer of money and the transfer of risk. Simple, right? This transaction saved AIG shareholders $500,000,000 in lost share value and prevented the loss of the AIG "AAA" status that it needed for all of its insurance bonds and guarantees – but more on that later.

Instead of giving the executives of General Re a medal for devising this unique business saving strategy, Federal prosecutors claimed that this financial alchemy of turning liabilities and risk into assets and profits was somehow fraudulent, and that these fine upstanding executives should go to jail for five years instead of helping other companies bolster their balance sheets as was done with AIG. Thankfully, the Second Circuit overturned the ridiculous convictions of these fine executives, whose only crime was coming up with a creative way to help its client, AIG, preserve its "AAA" rating. They actually saved AIG shareholders hundreds of Millions of dollars – instead of defrauding them – which is a preposterous result that only a "Spitzeresque" Federal prosecutor could consider fraud. They actually "saved" AIG without a taxpayer-funded bailout.

But it was Spitzer that forced AIG's Board of Directors to oust Mr. Greenberg from the Board of Directors and AIG in 2005. AIG had just entered the exciting world of insuring derivatives, and after Mr. Greenberg was forced out, the new management of AIG settled all claims of fraudulent accounting for $1.64 Billion. Note that amount is more than three times higher than the mere $500,000,000 that Goldman Sachs paid in fines for almost bringing down the entire economies of America and the Western World. For bolstering AIG's balance sheet in the terrible market of October 2000, Federal prosecutors wanted to crucify General Re executives Ronald Ferguson and Elizabeth Monrad, but no one at Goldman Sachs has been indicted for what they did to destroy AIG and the American economy.

While Mr. Greenberg was at AIG, he kept a firm hand on the burgeoning derivatives market and the insurance of those derivatives. After Mr. Greenberg was forced out, the inexperienced executives who took over had no idea what the rogue derivative traders were cooking up at offices in London and Connecticut. When AIG decided to go into the "lucrative" business of insuring "AAA" mortgage-backed securities that could not possibly go bad, legendary hedge fund investor John Paulson conspired with "Fabulous Fab" of Goldman Sachs to defraud not just other Goldman Sachs investors but American investors across the country. Mr. Paulson made Billions at the American taxpayers' expense because of his insider trading at Goldman Sachs. Since rigging the markets and defrauding the American taxpayers, Mr. Paulson's hedge fund has had nothing but one embarrassing loss after another and one losing year after another. But no one was indicted in that "insider trading" scandal that destroyed American and European banks and resulted in the "Great Recession."

Goldman Sachs not only convinced AIG to insure its bad mortgage portfolios, but soon AIG became the insurer of everyone's bad mortgages. Several books have done a great job explaining how the toxic mortgage market was created, but the only game in town to insure that toxic mortgage ilk was AIG, and that was because of the seduction of naïve managers at AIG by the crafty con artists at Goldman that convinced AIG to insure Trillions of toxic mortgages for pennies on the dollar. The only way this could happen in 2007, is that Eliot Spitzer forced Mr. Greenberg out of AIG in 2005, yet no one at AIG or Goldman Sachs has been prosecuted for the destruction of the American economy or the American housing market.

Had Glass-Steagall not been repealed in 1999, the carnage would not have been as great, but still Lehman Brothers and Bear Stearns would have gone down. The contagion that took down the major banks and jeopardized American investors and depositors was caused by the prospective failure of AIG. Goldman Sachs convinced its former Chairman, Treasury Secretary Hank Paulson – also a Paulson (but no relation) – to have the Government put in over $260 Billion to save AIG – and of that amount over $60-70 Billion went directly to Goldman Sachs to "insure" or bail out all of Goldman Sachs' toxic mortgage securities. So, because of Goldman's fraud and perfidy, $260 Billion of Main Street's money went to prop up Wall Street bankers and their wives, and most of all, Goldman Sachs.

There is no better story on how Wall Street executives took advantage of the American taxpayer than investigative reporter Matt Taibbi's article in <u>Rolling Stone Magazine</u> "The Real Housewives of Wall Street" (April 12, 2011) that explains how a couple of the Wall Street executives' wives with no business experience received $220 Million in loans from the Federal government in TARP money and stimulus money at almost zero interest. Furthermore, Goldman Sachs received almost $800 Billion in near zero interest loans from the same program that could have been used to pay off **all** student loan indebtedness for every college graduate. Similarly, Morgan Stanley received over TWO TRILLION DOLLARS in near zero interest loans. It would have been better for the Government to pay off each and every one of the foreclosed mortgages across the country, pay off all college graduate student loan debt, and offer free healthcare to everyone. It is not your imagination if you think Wall Street is getting rich while American wealth plummets.

Had Eliot Spitzer not gone after Mr. Greenberg of AIG, the Federal prosecutors would not have gone after the executives of General Re and "Finite Reinsurance" could still be used to this day to bolster the balance sheets of other companies. Had Spitzer not forced the AIG Board to get rid of Mr. Greenberg, the derivative crew in London could not have gone wild and started writing guarantees for mortgage portfolios that sharp hedge fund managers would blow up in a matter of time. Remember, insurance is supposed to be boring, and you can only buy it when you really do not need it. Here, Goldman Sachs was buying fire insurance at ridiculously low prices and no one saw that each of the mortgages was doused in gasoline and came with a pack of matches with each portfolio. AIG was now in the business of insuring mortgages that were not guaranteed to be paid off, but rather, were guaranteed to default. It was only a matter of time before these securities would blow up. Not a question of "if," but when. The iconic Hank Greenberg never would have allowed that, and would not have been conned and suckered by Goldman Sachs.

But, Hank Greenberg was gone. Eliot Spitzer forced him out just as Mr. Greenberg's sons were forced out and made to become the CEOs of other insurance companies. No one was left to protect the shareholders and employees of AIG. Ronald Ferguson and Elizabeth Monrad had been wrongfully indicted and prosecuted. The AIG family lost Billions, the American family lost Trillions, and numerous banks failed across America, and the wealth of the average American family was cut in half from $126,000 in 2007 as the crisis was just starting and the stock market and housing market were at their peaks, to the 1984-1990 level of $77,000. All of this loss, all of this destruction of American wealth, was because of the greed, vanity, and reckless political ambition of one man – Eliot Spitzer.

As Justice Louis Brandeis warned us:

"The greatest dangers to liberty lurk in insidious encroachment by men of zeal, well meaning but without understanding." *Olmstead v. United States,* 277 U.S. 438 (1928)

CHAPTER THIRTEEN
THE CHARTER OAK AFFAIR

Midnight, Sunday May 1st, 2011, Americans every-where cheered the President's announcement that two dozen Navy SEALs raided Osama bin Laden's compound in Pakistan, in the early morning hours of May 2nd Pakistan time, and successfully dispatched the Al Qaeda leader while seizing his computer information. Less than a month later on May 26, 2011, 78 heavily armed Federal Agents in Kevlar vests and with auto-matic weapons drawn raided the offices of the Charter Oak Trust in a small town in Connecticut. The Federal Agents herded the employees like cattle into several different conference rooms; threatening certain employees who were questioning what the Federal Agents were doing, and causing several women to faint and have ambulances to be called to revive them and tend to them. The Federal Agents stayed for more than 20 hours, taking hundreds of boxes of documents and over one Terabyte of computer ESI – Electronically Stored Information and emails.

The President is very proud of his "taking out" of Osama bin Laden and seizing bin Laden's computer. He intends to make the killing of bin Laden a major part of his campaign for re-election. However, what Americans should really be asking is: "Why did you need to raid the offices of the Charter Oak Trust? Why couldn't you have had someone from the IRS, DOL, or even the FBI just serve a subpoena or a summons on the receptionist at the offices that were raided?" Especially since this was the **Second Time** that the offices of the Charter Oak Trust were raided using the Government's favorite tool of search and seizure: the sealed search warrant. The very same offices had been raided on April 20, 2010 by 72 heavily armed federal agents in Kevlar vests and with automatic weapons drawn. The first raid was conducted by the IRS Criminal Investigation Division led by – you guessed it – Special Agent Commando Shaun Schrader – using a sealed search warrant issued out of the U.S. Attorney's Office of Milwaukee, Wisconsin, despite the fact that the Charter Oak Trust did no business in Wisconsin. The IRS-CID illegally and inappropriately seized several hundred boxes of documents and personal property – virtually none of which has been returned to its rightful owners since that time despite a Federal Judge's order to the contrary – and so much Electronically Stored Information (ESI) and emails that the Assistant U.S. Attorney (AUSA) involved requested to use a "taint team" of a dozen IRS Agents to go through a mountain of emails because if it was stacked up, "it would be taller than the Sears Tower in Chicago." Obviously there were no tall buildings in Milwaukee that could do "justice" to the AUSA's analogy. Despite having all of the materials illegally seized pursuant to a facially defective sealed search warrant filled with material misrepresentations, the materials have not been returned, nor has the taint team finished its review of all of the emails and ESI illegally seized.

This is the same IRS-CID that the President says he wants to hire 16,000 new agents to run and monitor compliance with the President's new healthcare plan and 4,000 new agents to go after wealthy taxpayers and put them through an audit from Hell. For example, how would you like your daughter to be served a summons by two large IRS-CID Special Agents on her college campus? Imagine that they show up at her dorm room at 7:00 in the morning, just like at Denise Simon's house. They serve her with a summons to be interviewed concerning **you and your** – her father's – tax affairs, which of course your child knows absolutely nothing about. After all, how many college students know anything about their parents' financial affairs – much less tax returns? Now, how would you feel if the first words out of the IRS-CID Agents' mouths during your daughter's interview are: "You know your father is a liar and thief don't you? You know your father is a tax cheat? You must know that don't you?"

Your daughter is being brow-beaten by two burly IRS-CID Special Agents – and you are out of town on business and your family attorney, who is there to protect your daughter, does not stop the IRS interviewer because he just wants your daughter to get through this, so she would not need to be subjected to a second interview. He has never experienced anything like this in his legal career of almost forty years. Your daughter broke down in tears as her father and family were ridiculed and accused of all sorts of scurrilous activities and tax evasion by the IRS-CID Special Agents.

You are saying two things to yourself right now: "This is America; this cannot possibly be a true story." It is totally true, and the entrepreneur this happened to has been audited several times with no change in his tax returns, which all were done by a conservative small-town Midwest accounting firm. He happens to be in the solar and wind alternative energy business that the President seems to heavily favor for the future. But this is what the President wants to do to all small businessmen. Not Apple, not GE, but your small business. No one from the IRS-CID has brow-beaten the daughter of the President's fundraising friend at Solyndra or raided the offices of Goldman Sachs.

The second thought you are having is if the IRS-CID already knows so much about you that they can make these outrageous accusations about you to your own daughter, why do they need to interview your daughter? After all, they had already summonsed thousands of pages of documents from your accountants and your business partners; what could they possibly learn from your daughter? Why would the President's administration do this to an American family? After all, the IRS-CID Special Agents that threatened **your** daughter and killed Denise Simon all work for the same President that killed bin Laden.

The answer to that question comes from a regional manager of the EPA that was speaking to a group of oil executives – in Texas no less – and explained the way that the President's new administration would make up for the lax regulatory environment of the eight years of the Bush (43) administration by using what he described as the "Roman way" of managing the territories it conquered. As Regional EPA Manager Al Armendariz explained, the Romans would come into a new territory, pick five or six locals and crucify them. By doing so, it made the future management of the province that much easier.

His actual statement was:

The Romans used to conquer little villages in the Mediterranean. They'd go into a little Turkish town somewhere, they'd find the first five guys they saw and they would crucify them. And then, you know, that town was really easy to manage for the next few years.

So the President's Administration campaign will be to insist on using the power of the federal government to "shock and awe" American citizens and American small businesses to do business their way or risk that you will be "crucified" in the public square; or your business will be raided; or your daughter will receive the "third degree" from the IRS-CID; and if nothing else they will handcuff you in front of your children or your employees, and even cause your wife to commit suicide. Instead of water-boarding terrorists, the President's Administration will "water-board" American tax-payers. The President has ordered the killing of American citizens, what will stop him from using the Commerce Clause to make you buy health insurance or do anything else the Administration wants you to do in the name of the greater good. Please remember, the Commerce Clause was meant to regulate inter-state commerce, not American citizens. But, see for example, the pride the President took in having 475 small healthcare businesses raided for $450,000,000 of Medicare fraud. That is a very small drop in a very large $80 Billion a year Medicare fraud bucket.

We will discuss the President's plan for healthcare elsewhere in this book. But suffice it to say, if the President and his regulators and administrators plan to use the IRS-CID Special Agents and Sealed Search Warrants to investigate "tax-dodgers" under the new healthcare law and use the "crucifixion" techniques of the EPA to regulate both business and the economy as well as the delivery of healthcare, you can now understand why almost TWO THOUSAND AMERICANS renounce their American citizenship each year to escape the "Gestapo" tactics of the IRS-CID and the "crucifixion" tactics of the President's administration and regulators. The President wants to hire 16,000 new Special Agents to monitor and regulate his "affordable" healthcare plan, and 4,000 IRS Special Agents to raid the homes and businesses of the wealthy. Are we really that far away from Greek-style riots in the streets, higher taxes, austerity budgets and devalued currency?

So the only rationale that can be assumed for the President's tactics in regulating small businesses is that the President means to rule by example and use the powers of the IRS, DOL and FBI and sealed search warrants to keep every small business living in fear so that no one dares to defy the tax man or the most powerful government on earth.

But why did the President need to raid the Charter Oak Trust twice, once on April 20, 2010 with 72 armed federal agents from the IRS-CID and then again on May 26, 2011 with 78 armed federal agents from the DOL and FBI? Why did the President need to send three times the number of federal agents that took out Osama bin Laden to do an armed commando raid on the offices of a trust in a small town in Connecticut when certainly an accountant with glasses could have easily served the receptionist with a summons or subpoena? Perhaps someday, when the "sealed" search warrant affidavit is unsealed, we will learn at that time what the alleged probable cause was for the issuance of a sealed search warrant and an armed commando raid on a small American village. The President is fond of reminding people that he went to Harvard. Perhaps he read Kafka's The Trial there and can understand the frustration of small business taxpayers who are invaded by the IRS-CID every day with the use of sealed search warrants. This is happening every day in the President's America.

But what is the Charter Oak Trust? Some terrorist feeder-fund organization? No; far from it. The Charter Oak Trust is a welfare benefit plan as described under IRC Section 419(e) that purchased 87 insurance policies on 84 insured participants from January 2007 to December 2009. That means on two separate occasions there were hundreds of boxes of documents and computers and huge amounts of ESI illegally seized by armed commandos – almost one armed federal agent for each insured participant in the Charter Oak Trust. When did life insurance in a welfare benefit plan become illegal in America?

The President's Administration is conducting a war on life insurance inside a welfare benefit plan. With the Charter Oak Trust, there is no tax deduction, and the AUSA in charge of the case in the U.S. Attorney's Office in New Haven, Connecticut refuses to divulge what possible crime a fully-insured welfare benefit plan could possibly be guilty of or why over 160 federal agents from three federal agencies and over $1,000,000 of the taxpayers' money should be used to carry out these commando raids on a small trust on two separate occasions.

The irony of the two different commando raids is that after the first raid of April 20, 2010, the administrators of the Charter Oak Trust had to order new policies because the Government seized the **original** life insurance policies and refused to return them despite the fact that copies would be as good as originals in court; as if a life insurance policy contract could possibly be evidence of any crime. But that did not stop the Government from illegally seizing the newly issued 87 policies a second time during the raid of May 26, 2011. This raid, carried out by the DOL and FBI at the behest of the U.S. Attorney's Office in New Haven, also refuses to return the original 87 Charter Oak Trust policies or explain why there was a second commando raid on the Charter Oak Trust. But having learned from dealing with the U.S. Attorney's Office in Milwaukee from the first commando raid of April 20, 2010, this time the attorneys for the administrators of the Charter Oak Trust told the Federal Judge that instead of having a new "taint team" review all of the illegally seized materials, the Charter Oak Trust would give the Judge copies of the 87 life insurance applications, so the Court could review them for any misrepresentations or illegalities, in exchange for the return of all of the illegally seized property. Surprisingly, and to the AUSA's chagrin, the Judge said there was no need for a taint team to review the hundreds of boxes because he would be willing to review all of the insurance applications – *in camera* – meaning in his court under his review. Suffice it to say, no taint team was created, no documents were reviewed, and over a year later the property illegally seized has not been returned including the 87 original life insurance policies, nor has the "sealed" search warrant been unsealed despite the efforts of the attorneys for the administrators of the Charter Oak Trust, despite the promises of the AUSA to the contrary or the Fourth

Amendment to the Constitution of the United States.

Since the President was a former law student at Harvard and a former Professor of Constitutional Law, he will probably recall these immortal words by one of the greatest Supreme Court Justices of all time – Justice Louis Brandeis – in his condemnation of the Government's unreasonable search and seizure violations of every American's Constitutional rights under the Fourth Amendment in cases like the two raids on the Charter Oak Trust:

Unjustified search and seizure violates the Fourth Amendment, whatever the character of the paper; whether the paper when taken by the federal officers was in the home, **in an office,** or elsewhere; whether the taking was effected by force, by fraud, or in the orderly process of a court's procedure. From these decisions, it follows necessarily that the Amendment is violated by the officer's reading the paper without a physical seizure, without his even touching it, and that use, in any criminal proceeding, of the contents of the paper so examined – as where they are testified to by a federal officer who thus saw the document, or where, through knowledge so obtained, a copy has been procured elsewhere – **any such use constitutes a violation of the Fifth Amendment.**

The protection guaranteed by the Amendments is much broader in scope. **The makers of our Constitution undertook to secure conditions favorable to the pursuit**

of happiness. They recognized the significance of man's spiritual nature, of his feelings, and of his intellect. They knew that only a part of the pain, pleasure and satisfactions of life are to be found in material things. They sought to protect Americans in their beliefs, their thoughts, their emotions and their sensations. They conferred, as against the Government, the right to be let alone – the most comprehensive of rights, and the right most valued by civilized men. To protect that right, every unjustifiable intrusion by the Government upon the privacy of the individual, whatever the means employed, must be deemed a violation of the Fourth Amendment.

And the use, as evidenced in a criminal proceeding, of facts ascertained by such intrusion must be deemed a violation of the Fifth. Olmstead v. United States, 277 U.S. 438, 477-79 (1928) (Brandeis, J.) (emphasis added).

Please reread that section with Justice Brandeis' comments on the "pursuit of happiness" again. You should be very concerned about your civil liberties and your future. All we can add to this is that if the police powers of the President and the Executive Branch are being used to "crucify" small insured welfare benefit plans that only have 84 participants in them, who will protect you if the Supreme Court rules that the Commerce Clause can be used to force you to buy health insurance – or anything else the Government deems fit and proper. What next? Can the Government force you to buy life insurance as well? The IRS-CID, DOL, and FBI are waiting patiently outside your door – ready to raid your house, your business, and "interview" your daughter. What does the Government need to do so that you will wake up? Water-board your wife? Cut off Social Security and Medicare to your mother? Handcuff your best friend and take him away to be "interviewed" for **your** private tax matters? The President's Administration is at war with life insurance in welfare benefit plans, oil, coal, and natural gas and private health insurance companies. How long will it be before the IRS-CID shows up at **your** door because you do not wish to purchase health insurance because it has doubled or tripled in cost due to the President's new law? If the President would send 24 federal agents to kill Osama bin Laden, and six times that number to kill the Charter Oak Trust, do you really feel safe in America? When a black Harvard professor was improperly arrested by a Boston police officer, the President invited both men to the Rose Garden for beers. Mr. President: The administrators of the Charter Oak Trust are patiently waiting for their invitation to the Rose Garden for beers, wine or cocktails. The wine will be our treat, Mr. President. There are some things going on in America – illegal acts by people in your administration that you need to hear about. If you need our address, just ask the Commissioner of the IRS, the Secretary of Labor or the

Justice Department. They all have our address, and they have all been to our offices several times. And, by the way, an invitation in the U.S. Mail is perfectly fine. We are big fans of the Postal Service. You should be funding the Postal Service rather than General Motors, Goldman Sachs and the War in Afghanistan. In fact, you could fund the annual deficit of the U.S. Postal Service with the Six Billion Dollars in fraudulent tax refunds the IRS sends out each year. No reason to have hand delivery by armed commandos working for the IRS-CID or the FBI. Thank you in advance for your attention to this matter.

CHAPTER FOURTEEN
THE SECTION 6708 AFFAIR

How many jobs were created by the American Jobs Creation Act (AJCA) of October 22, 2004? Not many – if any at all. Probably none. The only thing for sure is that the AJCA created a whole series of new income tax penalties that the National Taxpayer Advocate called "unconscionable if not unconstitutional" in her 2008 report to Congress. As the best proof yet that no one in Congress reads the tax bills they pass, the AJCA created multi-Million dollar penalties for small businesses that are non-appealable and non-reviewable even by a Federal Court. So that means that all of the Senators that voted for the AJCA ignored the checks and balances system of the Framers of the Constitution going all the way back to *Marbury v. Madison,* U.S. (1 Cranch) 137, 177 (1803) and created a law that would allow a mere IRS Revenue Agent, without the benefit of any hearing or due process, to assess multi-Million dollar penalties against individuals and businesses that cannot be reviewed by a Federal Judge or even by your Congressman or Senator. And if you think that is extreme, wait until you see the new tax penalties under the other bill that no one in Congress bothered to read; the President's "affordable" healthcare bill.

There is no question that these series of laws and their penalties are unconstitutional as written and someday they will be overturned as soon as the Supreme Court reviews them. The Draconian penalties passed in the AJCA show how mindless regulations (e.g. see new Code Section 409A) combined with huge penalty assessments can destroy any type of employee benefit plan. The AJCA was passed to deal with egregious tax shelters like BOSS and Son of BOSS and the law firms and accounting firms (so-called "material advisors") promoting them, but instead the only penalties levied to date on taxpayers have been for life insurance in pension plans and life insurance in welfare benefit plans. IRS Agents have not fined any of the large tax shelters that annually generate Billions of dollars of tax savings and deductions for Apple, Google, GE and other major companies so they pay little or no taxes on Billions of dollars of earnings. But they have fined doctors and other small businessmen with $800,000 fines that are totally non-appealable for allegedly participating in a "listed transaction" in 2002 or 2003 that became a "reportable transaction" by definition for transactions only after August 3, 2007.

You will probably have a difficult time believing that what you are about to read could happen in the America that you know and love, but we will provide you with indisputable evidence that everything you are about to read is the 100% fully documented, unadulterated truth. We also know that you are already thinking "how could the imposition of these multi-Million dollar fines for prior conduct not violate the Excessive Fines Clause, or the Bill of Attainder and Ex Post Facto clauses of the Constitution?" Don't worry, we will get to that in due course.

When Section 6708 was amended by the AJCA in October 2004, the penalty for the failure to maintain a list of material advisees by a "material advisor" was $50 per advisee up to a maximum penalty of $50,000 per calendar year. The new penalty under Section 6708 was raised to $10,000 per day for failure to turn over a list to the IRS for years after October 23, 2004 with no maximum; so after four months, the IRS Agent could penalize an individual or a small business $1,200,000 for failing to turn over a list, and this penalty would not be reviewable by anyone including a Federal Judge, the Commissioner of the IRS, Senator Grassly, Senator Baucus, Senator Reed, or even the President of the United States. No, we are not kidding. Read the Code Section for yourself. Obviously, your Congressman or Senator did not read it before it was passed. It is clearly unconstitutional.

I should know because I have had to become the leading authority on Section 6708 since I – and the welfare benefit plans that I created – and its sponsors, are the only entities in the entire country that have been penalized under the new Section 6708 of the Tax Code since the Regulations under the new Section 6708 became final on August 3, 2007. How do I know that?

Our inquiries to the office of the National Taxpayer Advocate resulted in the disclosure of a recent report published by the United States Government Accountability Office (GAO) on <u>Abusive Tax Avoidance Transactions</u> (the "GAO Report") (May 2011). The Report raises some very disturbing statistics over the Government's handling of the 26 U.S.C. § 6708 penalties assessed against the Carpenter entities. The troubling findings contained in the GAO Report, made by one of the major and perhaps most reliable agencies of the entire Federal government, the Government Accountability Office, should give you serious pause regarding the Government's actions. But the most shocking statistic in the GAO Report is found on page 40, where it states that the **total** number of penalty assessments under Section 6708 for the year 2009 was **five** for a grand total of $4,840,000 – **all** of which were assessed against your author and the various entities in the welfare benefit plan business. Neither I nor any of the penalized entities are "material advisors" or involved in any type of abusive tax shelter business, but we have been fined by an ordinary IRS agent for almost $5,000,000 in punitive penalties without any trial, hearing or due process of any sort. Mr. President, when can we meet in the Rose Garden to discuss how people in **your** Administration are violating the Constitutional rights of ordinary Americans every day? As a former professor of Constitutional Law, you should be very interested in the rest of this Chapter.

There were no assessments in 2008 or 2010 under Section 6708, and the three assessments made in 2007 under the past administration were virtually all abated by the Government. Likewise in 2005, there were **no assessments** whatsoever under the new Section 6708 law passed as part of the American Jobs Creation Act of October 22, 2004 ("AJCA"). Interestingly enough, the **four** assessments in 2006 amounted to only $2,600 and those fines were paid in their entirety by the offending "material advisors." Other than the **five** penalties assessed against the Carpenter related entities in 2009, no other "material advisors" or "reportable transactions" have been penalized since the IRS published requirements for both a "material advisor" and a "reportable transaction" becoming effective for reportable transactions after August 3, 2007.

Those requirements are:

A. There must be a reportable transaction;

B. That the person made a tax statement about;

C. That induced the taxpayer to enter into that reportable transaction; and

D. The person was paid the threshold amount for making the tax statement.

Treas. Reg. § 301.6111-3(b)(4).

Similarly, see, Reg. § 301.6112-1(g), which states as to "reportable" transactions:

This section applies to transactions with respect to which a material advisor makes a tax statement on or after August 3, 2007. (Emphasis added).

In other words; to be a "material advisor" you must be paid the "threshold amount" of $250,000 for writing a legal opinion (tax statement) that induces a taxpayer to enter an abusive tax shelter (reportable transaction). Think Jenkens & Gilchrist and the Son of Boss tax shelter. Jenkens & Gilchrist was routinely paid $500,000 by its clients for favorable legal opinions involving thousands of taxpayers in numerous abusive tax shelters.

But then we come to 2009, and more than three and a half years after receiving a letter request from an IRS Revenue Agent in January 2006 asking for their "material advisor" lists for the **calendar year 2002**, the only taxpayers in **the entire country** assessed under the new Section 6708 penalty under the AJCA of 2004 are your author and the Carpenter-affiliated welfare benefit plan entities. There are only five penalties assessed after 2007, after the new regulations for the new law came into the Tax Code, and we learn on Page 26 of the GAO Report that these five penalties range from a low of $740,000 to a high of $1,100,000, for a grand total of $4,840,000.

Who are these five unlucky people or entities? As the Government knows well by now, since 2009 both 419 Plan Services, Inc. and its Carpenter-related affiliates have been fighting the Government's improper liens against them for $1.1 Million each based on these "unconscionable and unconstitutional" penalties under Section 6708. (See Taxpayer Advocate 2008 Annual Report to Congress, Vol. 1, at 419-422.).

But all told, the IRS Agent assessed penalties of $1.1 Million against three entities including 419 Plan Services, Inc., and a $740,000 penalty against another of its affiliates -- which ceased operation at the end of the year 2000 and for which it had been replaced as Sponsor by another company in 2001. All four of these entities were hit with arbitrary and capricious penalties by the Agent for $740,000 to $1.1 Million each for allegedly being a material advisor in 2002 and not complying with the request for a list of material advisors in 2006. This total comes to $4.1 Million; and the missing $740,000 penalty belongs to the fifth penalized party, me, and the only amount collected by the Government as listed in the GAO Report was the $11,256 in tax refunds seized from my wife's tax return – which was not even a joint return.

In any event, failure to file a regular tax return might result in a $1,000 fine. Failure to file a 1099 Form or a K-1 informational return will result in a $50 a month fine, and the maximum penalty under Section 6700 (misrepresenting a tax shelter) would have been $1,000; and Section 6703(c) would have allowed the Section 6700 offender to pay 15% or $150 and entitled them to bring a refund claim in federal court. But, apparently, the Government believes people and entities should be fined over a Million dollars each for not turning over a "list" that they were never required to maintain as a matter of law.

The GAO Report itself says that non-"material advisors" **are not liable for maintaining a list** or for the **Section 6708 penalty**:

> Promoters who do not meet the statutory definition to be a material advisor face no requirements to provide IRS with their list of investors within 20 business days after IRS requested a list or **no penalties for failing to do so**. GAO Report pages 27-28 (emphasis added).

By targeting only Carpenter-affiliated fully-insured welfare benefit plans for Section 6708 penalties, and for assessing pre-2004 conduct with a post-2004 multi-Million dollar penalty where the definitions were not even finalized until after 2007, and for a period of time in which the requirements to impose such penalties did not even exist, the Government's actions clearly violate the Excessive Fines, Bill of Attainder, and Ex Post Facto Clauses of the Constitution. As a Harvard Law Scholar and a Constitutional Law professor, the President should know that, and you should hold him accountable this November. We will.

With the release of the Government Accountability Office Report (the "GAO Report") showing that of the 12 Section 6708 penalties assessed since the law changed under the American Jobs Creation Act ("AJCA") of October 22, 2004, the only remaining penalties are against your author and the four Carpenter-affiliated entities ranging from my $740,000 up to the $1.1 Million penalties for the related entities, for a total of $4.8 Million. The remaining

$740,000 against the last Carpenter-affiliated entity just shows the arbitrary and capricious nature of these assessments, as the Trust that was penalized by the errant IRS agent never existed.

Therefore, as I am sure you can clearly see, these egregious and unconscionable fines are the epitome of "arbitrary and capricious" and should be abated immediately before this becomes a national scandal. The IRS Agent sent his letter in January 2006 asking for a "list" that was not even defined or required by the AJCA until after August 3, 2007 when the new Regulations were first published. Please see the new Regulations under §6111 and §6112 for yourself. They both have language for only reportable transactions and material advisors after August 3, 2007. Moreover, the penalty assessment forms and the letters speak of conduct for the year ending December 31, 2002 – a full two years before the AJCA itself came into being on October 22, 2004 for years thereafter.

And as if that was not enough, the IRS Agent waited a full three and a half years in July 2009 to assess the penalties for a letter sent in January 2006 referencing conduct in 2002. None of these parties ever received a check for **$250,000** for writing a **legal opinion** that induced a **taxpayer** to enter a **reportable** transaction.

Since there were no Section 6708 penalty assessments in 2005, 2008 or 2010, and the four penalty assessments in 2006 were so small (only $2,400 in total) and the $1 Million penalties assessed in 2007 were all abated, fully half of the penalty assessments made since October 22, 2004 and 100% of the outstanding assessments made by this Administration have been made against the Carpenter-affiliated entities and myself. So your author wants to be firmly on record that the penalties assessed by the IRS Agent are not just arbitrary and capricious and erroneously assessed, they are also unconstitutional on their face because they violate the prohibitions of the Excessive Fines Clause, the Bill of Attainder Clause and the Ex Post Facto Clause of the United States Constitution.

The Excessive Fines Clause of the Eighth Amendment to the United States Constitution is implicated any time the Government "extract[s a] payment, whether in cash or in kind, 'as punishment for some offense.'" *Austin v. United States*, 509 U.S. 602, 609-610 (1993) (quoting *Browning-Ferris Indus. of Vt., Inc. v. Kelco Disposal, Inc.*, 492 U.S. 257, 265 (1989)). In 1998, the Supreme Court held that a punitive fine or forfeiture is "constitutionally excessive" if it is grossly disproportional to the gravity of the offense that it is designed to punish. *United States v. Bajakajian*,

524 U.S. 321, 334 (1998). Although Bajakajian involved a criminal forfeiture, the Court has previously held **punitive civil forfeitures** subject to the limitations of the Excessive Fines Clause. See, Austin, 509 U.S. at 602.

The Supreme Court set the standard for violation of the Excessive Fines Clause in *Bajakajian*:

Respondent Hosep Bajakajian attempted to leave the United States without reporting, as required by federal law, that he was transporting more than $10,000 in currency. Federal law also provides that a person convicted of willfully violating this reporting requirement shall forfeit to the Government "any property ... involved in such offense." 18 U.S.C. § 982(a)(1). The question in this case is whether forfeiture of the entire $357,144 that respondent failed to declare would violate the Excessive Fines Clause of the Eighth Amendment.

We hold that it would, because full forfeiture of respondent's currency would be grossly disproportional to the gravity of his offense. Id. at 324.

The Supreme Court went on to explain the nature of the Excessive Fines Clause:

The Eighth Amendment provides: "Excessive bail shall not be required, nor excessive fines imposed, nor cruel and unusual punishments inflicted." U.S. Const., Amdt. 8. We have, however, explained that at the time the Constitution was adopted, "the word 'fine' was understood to mean a payment to a sovereign as punishment for some offense." Browning-Ferris Industries of Vt., Inc. v. Kelco Disposal, Inc., 492 U.S. 257, 265, 109 S.Ct. 2909, 2915, 106 L.Ed.2d 219 (1989). The Excessive Fines Clause thus "limits the government's power to extract payments, whether in cash or in kind, 'as punishment for some offense.'" Austin v. United States, 509 U.S. 602, 609-610, 113 S.Ct. 2801, 2805, 125 L.Ed.2d 488 (1993) (emphasis deleted). Forfeitures-payments in kind-are thus "fines" if they constitute punishment for an offense. *Id.* at 327-28.

In the present case, there is no doubt that a fine of $1.1 Million violates the Excessive Fines Clause for failure to file. What is tantamount to an informational only tax return, if that, and because there is no return; is only a requirement for people who are so-called "material advisors" to maintain a list of those they have advised to make use of a tax shelter, and does not serve any possible goal of government:

Although the Government has asserted a loss of information regarding the amount of currency leaving the country, that loss would not be remedied by the Government's confiscation of [Bajakajian's] $357,144. The forfeiture in this case does not bear any of the hallmarks of traditional civil in rem forfeitures. The Government has not proceeded against the currency itself, but has instead sought and obtained a criminal conviction of respondent personally. The forfeiture serves no remedial purpose, is designed to punish the offender, and cannot be imposed upon innocent owners. *Id.* at 329, 331-32.

Therefore, the only thing left to determine is how much of a fine is reasonable and how much of a fine would be determined by the Court to be "excessive" under the facts:

The touchstone of the constitutional inquiry under the Excessive Fines Clause is the principle of proportionality: The amount of the forfeiture must bear some relationship to the gravity of the offense that it is designed to punish. See Austin v. United States, 509 U.S., at 622-623, 113 S.Ct., at 2812 (noting Court of Appeals' statement that " 'the government is exacting too high a penalty in relation to the offense committed'"). Until today, however, we have not articulated a standard for determining whether a punitive forfeiture is constitutionally excessive. **We now hold that a punitive forfeiture violates the Excessive Fines Clause if it is grossly disproportional to the gravity of a defendant's offense.** Id. at 334 (emphasis added).

As Bajakajian's offense was for not filing a necessary report, his activity is exactly the same as in this case, with two major differences: Bajakajian **knew** that he had to file the currency report as all airline travelers must do, and he lied on the report that he was not carrying more than $10,000 of currency. In this case, the Carpenter-affiliated entities still claim that they never were "material advisors" and they said so in a letter to Revenue Agent Charles Clark in February 2006 that the Government admits it received.

Under this standard, the forfeiture of respondent's entire $357,144 would violate the Excessive Fines Clause. Respondent's crime was solely a reporting offense. It was permissible to transport the currency out of the country so long as he reported it. *Id.* at 337.

The harm that respondent caused was also minimal. **Failure to report his currency affected only one party, the Government, and in a relatively minor way.** There was no fraud on the United States, and respondent caused no loss to the public fisc. Had his crime gone undetected, the Government would have been deprived **only of the information** that $357,144 had left the country. Comparing the gravity of Bajakajian's crime with the [$1,100,000] [penalty] the Government seeks, we conclude that such a forfeiture would be grossly disproportional to the gravity of his offense. It is larger than the $5,000 fine imposed by the District

Court by many orders of magnitude, and it bears no articulable correlation to any injury suffered by the Government. *Id.* at 339-40 (emphasis added)

Therefore, clearly as applied to the Carpenter-affiliated welfare benefit plans, the Excessive Fines Clause has been violated. There is no possible logical determination other than "excessive" concerning this particular fine which has been called arbitrary, capricious, unconscionable and unconstitutional by people working in the Government, not just by your author.

Similarly, the Bill of Attainder Clause states: "No bill of attainder or ex post facto law shall be passed." U.S. Const., Art. I, § 9, cl. 3. A bill of attainder is "a law that legislatively determines guilt and **inflicts punishment upon an identifiable individual without provision of the protections of a judicial trial.**" *Nixon v. Adm'r of Gen. Servs.*, 433 U.S. 425,468 (1977) (emphasis added).

The Constitution's prohibition of bills of attainder was motivated by rejection of practices of the English Parliament, which periodically punished specifically designated persons or groups without trial. *United States v. Brown*, 381 U.S. 437, 447 (1965) (summarizing the basic history of bills of attainder). Although bills of attainder in the past identified persons by name for punishment, they may also include designations of groups of persons according to past conduct. *Selective Service System v. Minnesota Public Interest Research Group ("MPIRG"),* 486 U.S. 841, 847 (1984). The Bill of Attainder Clause not only protects individuals from legislative punishment or punishment by the executive branch of government, but also serves an important function in preserving the separation of powers. The Clause acts as "a general safeguard against legislative exercise of the judicial function, or more simply--trial by legislature." *Brown,* 381 U.S. at 442. To show that the Section 6708 penalty statute is unconstitutional as to the entities involved with the Benistar Trust, the Supreme Court has identified three requirements for a statute to qualify as an unconstitutional bill of attainder: specification of the affected persons; punishment; and lack of a meaningful judicial role. *MPIRG,* 468 U.S. at 847.

"A bill of attainder is a legislative act which inflicts punishment without a judicial trial." *Cummings v. Missouri,* 71 U.S. 281, 323 (1867). Such laws "subvert the presumptions of innocence, and... They assume that the parties are guilty..." *Id.* at 328. "Legislative acts, no matter what their form, that apply either to named individuals or to easily ascertainable members of a group in such a way as to inflict punishment on them without a judicial trial are bills of attainder prohibited by the Constitution." *Brown,* 381 U.S. at 448-49. The Supreme Court has made clear that any statute that imposes "sanctions on named or identifiable individuals would be immediately constitutionally suspect." *Nixon*, 433 U.S. at 473.

Because the federal government has only those powers that are specifically granted to it by the people through the Constitution, it has long been held that "an act of the legislature, repugnant to the constitution, is void." *Marbury v. Madison*, U.S. (1 Cranch) 137, 177 (1803) (Marshall, C.J., for a unanimous court); see, e.g., *Brown*, 81 U.S. at 462 (Congress "shall pass no bills of attainder, no ex post facto laws, and the like. Limitations of this kind can be preserved in practice no other way than through the medium of the courts of justice; whose duty it must be to declare all acts contrary to the manifest tenor of the constitution void. *Chicago, I. & L.R. Co. v. Hackett*, 228 U.S. 559, 566 (1913) (an unconstitutional law is "as inoperative as if it had never been passed"); *Ex Parte Siebold*, 100 U.S. 371, 376 (1880) (a law repugnant to the Constitution "is void, and is as no law"); see also, *St. Joseph Stock Yards Co. v. United States*, 298 U.S. 38, 52 (1936) ("Under our system there is no warrant for the view that the judicial power of a competent court can be circumscribed by administrative action going beyond the limits of constitutional authority.")

As Justice Scalia concisely explained, "what a court does with regard to an unconstitutional law is simply to ignore it." *Reynoldsville Casket Co. v. Hyde*, 514 U.S. 749, 760 (1995) (Scalia, J., concurring). Did the President not **read** or **teach** any of Justice Scalia's opinions on the Constitutionality of laws and regulations? Although the unenforceability of an unconstitutional law was a question settled decisively at the outset of the Republic by Chief Justice Marshall in the landmark decision of *Marbury v. Madison*, 5 U.S. 137 (1803), a way around Marbury appears to be precisely what the Government seeks here. The Government is essentially asking to make some sort of exception to the ordinary principles of Constitutional Law and allow this unconstitutional penalty to be used to punish the people in this case. More than 200 years ago, Chief Justice Marshall heard and, on behalf of a unanimous Supreme Court, rejected the identical plea:

> If an act of the legislature, repugnant to the constitution, is void, does it, notwithstanding its invalidity, bind the courts, and oblige them to give it effect? Or, in other words, though it not be law, does it constitute a rule as operative as if it was a law? This would overthrow in fact what was established in theory; and would seem, at first view, an absurdity too gross to be insisted upon. *Id.* at 177.

This attempt to retroactively fill in the gaps when no constitutionally-enacted definition of "material advisors," "reportable transactions," or the "list requirements" was in place simply to single out a group of individuals and entities for multi-Million dollar punishments is likewise "too gross to be insisted upon."

In the language of the Supreme Court, such a designation or label is "void;" it is "as no law;" it is "as inoperative as if it had never been passed," and it must be "ignored." The Secretary of the Treasury cannot make unconstitutional designations, just as Congress cannot pass unconstitutional laws, and the Judicial Branch has no Constitutional authority to legislate in the course of rendering its decisions. See also *Cummings*, 71 U.S. at 323-24 (discussing Earl of Kildare attainder); *BellSouth Corp. v. FCC,* 144 F.3d 58, 64 (D.C. Cir. 1998) (describing this as a "classic" bill of attainder).

Just as Henry VIII's edict made all who previously had rendered aid to the Earl of Kildare criminals, the Secretary of the Treasury's retroactive designation of certain people as "material advisors" made criminals of those who previously had aided and abetted "abusive tax shelters" at a time when there was no valid designation of the terms "material advisor" or "reportable transaction," and aiding and abetting even "abusive" tax shelters was not frowned upon, much less subject to multi-Million dollar fines. The times may have changed but the name for this singling out and declaring specific classes of persons criminal remains the same. Those laws are called "bills of attainder."

Time after time, the Supreme Court has struck down laws like these which punish persons for having provided support to some person or group who has fallen out of favor, such as Confederates or Communists. See also *Crain v. City of Mountain Home*, 611 F.2d 726, 729 (8th Cir. 1979) (striking down a city ordinance as bill of attainder that reduced salary of one named employee and removed another from office); *Steinberg v. United States*, 163 F. Supp. 590, 592 (Ct. Cl. 1958) (invalidating a bill of attainder that terminated pensions to federal employees who had asserted their Fifth Amendment right against self-incrimination.)

The same result should befall the Government's efforts today to label specific classes of entities as tax shelters, reportable transactions or listed transactions, and to punish those who previously had given them support as material advisors many years earlier. Once again, neither your author nor the welfare benefit entities ever participated in a "reportable transaction" or an abusive tax shelter, much less wrote a legal opinion or a tax statement for one. This sort of singling out of specifically named individuals to punish them for conduct already committed reflects an infamous history that the Framers decisively broke away from when ratifying the Constitution. As the GAO Report makes clear, there are far fewer "material advisors" that have been penalized under §6708 than Communists, Confederate sympathizers, and even actual terrorist group sympathizers living in the United States today that have been protected by the Supreme Court striking down Bill of Attainder laws over the past 150 years.

The specification requirement is satisfied when the statute either identifies individuals by name or as ascertainable members of a group based on past conduct. *MPIRG*, 468 U.S. at 847. A statute targeting groups based on past conduct can be a bill of attainder when the conduct "serves as 'a point of reference for the ascertainment of particular persons ineluctably designated by the legislature' for punishment." *Id.* (quoting *Communist Party of the United States v. Subversive Activities Control Bd.*, 367 U.S. 1, 86 (1961).)

Courts have identified several "guideposts" to help determine whether the specification requirement has been met. See, e.g., *SeaRiver Maritime Fin. Holdings v. Mineta*, 309 F.3d 662, 669 (9th

Cir. 2002). One guidepost is whether the statute targets individuals or a class based on past conduct which operates as a designation of particular persons. *MPIRG*, 468 U.S. at 847; *SeaRiver Maritime*, 309 F.3d at 670. It is uncontested that the individuals in this case affected by the § 6708 penalties are determined by their past acts (or more accurately, by their past failures to act). Another guidepost is whether the past conduct consists of "irreversible acts." *MPIRG*, 468 U.S. at 848; *SeaRiver Maritime*, 309 F.3d at 671. Here again, the specific group is "material advisors" and especially those associated with fully-insured welfare benefit plans (less than a dozen people nationwide), and the § 6708 penalty is for having not sent in a list of material advisees in February 2006 instead of sending a letter stating that none of the accused were, in fact, "material advisors" to begin with subject to the list maintenance requirement.

Whether the group is "easily ascertainable" is yet another way to judge the specification requirement. *Brown*, 381 U.S. at 448-49; *SeaRiver Maritime*, 309 F.3d at 669. The phrase "easily ascertainable" was introduced by the Court in *United States v. Lovett*, 328 U.S. 303, 315 (1946). In *Cummings v. Missouri*, 71 U.S. 277 (1866), the Court stated that bills of attainder, though "generally directed against individuals by name," may also "be directed against a whole class." *Id.* at 323. In *Lovett*, the Court held that unconstitutional bills of attainder apply "either to named individuals or to easily ascertainable members of a group." *Lovett*, 328 U.S. at 315. In this case, the Supreme Court would clearly have both in that "material advisors" are the "Communists" or the "Confederate sympathizers" that are the class of people being punished without trial, and more exclusively the Government is **only** prosecuting people associated with the Carpenter-affiliated fully-insured welfare benefit plans. This is a classic Bill of Attainder situation.

It is beyond peradventure that an extraordinary multi-Million dollar fine is punitive in nature and should be considered "punishment" in anyone's opinion. The early writings against Bills of Attainder all mention the word "penalty" specifically. Deciding whether a statute imposes punishment entails three inquiries: "(1) whether the challenged statute falls within the historical meaning of legislative punishment; (2) whether the statute, 'viewed in terms of the type and severity of burdens imposed, reasonably can be said to further non punitive legislative purposes'; and (3) whether the legislative record 'evinces a congressional intent to punish.'" *MPIRG*, 468 U.S. at 852 (quoting *Nixon*, 433 U.S. at 473, 475-76, 478). To constitute a bill of attainder, a statute need not evidence all three of these factors. *SeaRiver Maritime*, 309 F.3d at 673; see also Nixon, 433 U.S. at 475 (finding that "new burdens and deprivations" - those not within the historical meaning of punishment - also "might be legislatively fashioned that are inconsistent with the bill of attainder guarantee"). Nevertheless, here, all three factors are clearly embodied in this case. See, e.g., *Elgin v. United States*, 594 F. Supp. 2d 133 (D. Mass. 2009).

There is no conceivable manner in which due process could ever authorize a defendant to be punished under an unconstitutional law when no person ever had an opportunity to question its validity. See, e.g., *Yakus v. United States*, 321 U.S. 414, 447 (1944) ("Even though the statute should be deemed to require it, any ruling...that he had had no opportunity to establish the invalidity of the regulation by resort to the statutory procedure, would be reviewable on appeal on constitutional grounds."); *Estep v. United States*, 327 U.S. 114, 125 (1946) (Murphy, J., concurring) ("To...be [penalized and] punished without ever being accorded the opportunity to prove the prosecution is based upon an invalid administrative order...violates the most elementary and fundamental concepts of due process of law.").

It is not disputed that individuals and entities affected by the Section 6708 penalties in this case received no judicial evaluation before **or even after** being fined and penalized by Agent

Clark. Indeed, no judicial oversight at all or due process hearing has been provided to date, despite repeated representations by the Government that such due process hearing would be forthcoming shortly, but certainly no more than a few months time. The test for Bill of Attainder status, however, is whether the targeted individuals received a judicial trial before being penalized, not whether the legislature engaged directly in the implementation of the punishment or delegated it to the executive branch.

A multi-Million dollar civil penalty not only violates the "excessive fines" clause of the Eighth Amendment, it also most certainly constitutes a punitive fine or "punishment" that triggers the Ex Post Facto Clause of the Constitution. An ex post facto law is one which imposes a punishment for an act which was not punishable at the time it was committed, or a punishment in addition to that then prescribed. *Carpenter et. al. v. Commonwealth of Pennsylvania,* 17 How. 456 (1854) as cited in *Burgess v. Salmon,* 97 U.S. 381, 384 (1878).

An ex post facto law includes "[e]very law that makes an action done before the passing of the law, and which was innocent when done, criminal, and punishes such action." *Carmell v. Texas,* 29 U.S. 513, 522 (2000) (quoting *Calder v. Bull,* 3 U.S. (3 Dall.) 386, 390

(1798) (Chase, J.) (first of Calder's four types of ex post facto laws)). Quite simply, **"[l]egislatures may not retroactively alter the definition of crimes."** *Collins v. Youngblood*, 97 U.S. 37, 43 (1990) (emphasis added); see J. Nowak & R. Rotunda, Constitutional Law § 10.1 (4th ed. 1991) ("The ex post facto clauses effectively eliminate the ability of either the federal or state governments to punish persons for actions which were not illegal when performed."). Yet that is precisely what the Government has done here, by retroactively designating the Carpenter-affiliated welfare benefit plan as an abusive tax shelter or a reportable transaction by being substantially similar to a listed transaction in September 2010, and thereby penalizing any type of clerical support given to the welfare benefit plan in the past, and at a time when there was no valid law preventing the defendants from doing so. While the Government can make such conduct a crime going forward, the Ex Post Facto Clause precludes the Government – and all branches Government including all departments of the Executive Branch from doing so retroactively.

Unlike the Due Process Clause, the Ex Post Facto Clause is not subject to harmless error analysis. See *Landgraf v. USI Film Prods.*, 511 U.S. 244, 253 (1994) ("The Ex Post Facto Clause flatly prohibits retroactive application of penal legislation."). There is an "absolute prohibition" on ex post facto laws. *Schwab v. Doyle,* 258 U.S. 529, 534 (1922); see *NLRB v. Carlisle Lumber Co.,* 94 F. 138, 153 (9th Cir. 1937) (quoting *Doyle*); *United States v. Davis,* 397 F.3d 340, 348 (6th Cir. 2005) ("The ex post facto clause announces a fundamental constitutional absolute.") As Justice Douglas explained: "The Constitution places a ban on all ex post facto laws. There are no qualifications or exceptions. Article I, § 9, applicable to the Federal Government, speaks in absolute terms: 'No . . . ex post facto Law shall be passed.'" *Marcello v. Bonds,* 349 U.S. 302, 319 (1955) (Douglas, J., dissenting).

The Court of Appeals has clearly indicated that the Million dollar-plus penalty assessments in this case would constitute "punitive" fines that would trigger the Ex Post Facto Clause as a bar to the Government's actions in this case. In *Evans v. Gerry,* 647 F. 3d 30 (1st Cir. 2011), the First Circuit uses the Supreme Court formulation in *Calder v. Bull,* 3 U.S. 386 (1798), describing the four categories of laws that the Ex Post Facto Clause of the Constitution prohibits:

1st. Every law that makes an action done before the passing of the law, and which was innocent when done, criminal; and punishes such action. 2d. Every law that aggravates a crime, or makes it greater than it was, when committed. 3d. Every law that changes the punishment, and inflicts a greater punishment, than the law annexed to the crime, when committed. 4th. Every law that alters the legal rules of evidence, and receives less, or different, testimony, than the law required at the time of the commission of the offence, in order to convict the offender. *Evans v. Gerry*, 647 F. 3d 30, 32 (1st Cir. 2011).

The Ex Post Facto Clause "bars application of a law 'that changes the punishment, and inflicts a greater punishment, than the law annexed to the crime, when committed[.]' " Johnson v. United States, 529 U.S. 694, 699, (2000) (quoting Calder v. Bull, 3 U.S. 386, 390, (1798)) *Simmons v. Galvin,* 575 F.3d 24, 43, 57 (1st Cir. 2009).

This provision "forbids not only legislative creation of new criminal liability after the event but also a legislative increase in punishment after the event." United States v. Lata, 415 F.3d 107, 110 (1st Cir.2005). *Gonzales Fuentes v. Molina,* 607 F.3d 864, 876 (1st Cir. 2010).

Assuming that the Government would argue that a multi-Million dollar penalty for failure to respond to an IRS Agent's letter constitutes a "civil" penalty rather than a "punitive" fine, the First Circuit provides a very thorough and precise test. The First Circuit has established that the analysis of an Ex Post Facto Clause claim involves a two-part inquiry. The first asks whether the penalty is a civil, regulatory measure within the meaning of the case law, or whether it is punitive in nature:

"[W]here unpleasant consequences are brought to bear upon an individual for prior conduct," the central question "is whether the legislative aim was to punish that individual for past activity, or whether the restriction of the individual comes about as a relevant incident to a regulation of a present situation." De Veau v. Braisted, 363 U.S. 144, 160 (1960) (holding that state statutory bans against employment of convicted felons in certain jobs did not impose punishment under Ex Post Facto Clause). Only a punitive measure can violate the Ex Post Facto Clause. See, Smith v. Doe, 538 U.S. 84, 92, (2003). *Simmons v. Galvin*, 575 F.3d 24, 43 (1st Cir. 2009).

The first part asks whether the challenged law has a civil, regulatory purpose, or whether it is intended to punish. See Smith v. Doe, 538 U.S. 84, 92 (2002) (citing Kansas v. Hendricks, 521 U.S. 346, 361 (1997)). If a court finds that the law was intended to be punitive, then it constitutes "punishment" for purposes of the Ex Post Facto Clause and would violate the clause if retroactively applied. *Id.* However, if the law conveys a non-punitive, regulatory purpose, the court moves to the second part of the test to ascertain whether the law is "so punitive either in purpose or effect as to negate [the state's] intention to deem it civil." *Id.* (quoting United States v. Ward, 448 U.S. 242, 248-49 (1980)). The ultimate question is "whether [the Section 6708 penalty] is intended to be, or by its nature necessarily is, criminal and punitive, or civil and remedial." *United States v. One Assortment of 89 Firearms*, 465 U.S. 354, 362 (1984).

Under the second prong of the Smith analysis, even if a clear punitive intent is not discernible for the challenged law, it would nevertheless constitute a criminal punishment subject to the Ex Post Facto Clause if the measure's effect is so punitive as to negate any intent to deem it civil. *Hendricks*, 521 U.S. at 361, (citing *Ward*, 448 U.S. at 248-49). Id. at 58, 61.

[But], even if the legislature intended to deem a particular law "civil," courts must further inquire whether "the statutory scheme was so punitive either in purpose or effect as to negate that intention." *United States v. Ward*, 448 U.S. 242, 248-49 (1980). Id. at 44.

Under the First Circuit's two-part analysis, there can be no question that a Million dollar-plus fine is punitive in nature and is a punishment that would trigger implication of the Ex Post Facto Clause. The Supreme Court also held that fines in the form of civil legislation might still trigger the Ex Post Facto Clause. See, e.g., *Karpa v. Commissioner,* 909 F.2d 784 (1990):

The Court has also warned, however, that the constitutional prohibition against ex post facto legislation may not be avoided by giving civil formto criminal legislation. See *Burgess v. Salmon,* 97 U.S. 381, 384 1878). In Burgess, the Court held that where federal legislation made it a criminal offense to distribute tobacco without a proper tax stamp, imposition of an additional tax on tobacco when the distributor had already paid the tax under the prior law would violate the ex post facto clause. The Court reasoned that to impose criminal punishment retroactively, or, alternatively, a "penalty" in the form of the increased tax, where "the one was equally authorized with the other," would violate the ex post facto clause. *Id. Karpa,* at 787.

The new Regulations clarifying the new rules under § 6112 were effective only for transactions after August 3, 2007. From 2003 until October 23, 2004, when the AJCA Code amendments became effective, "Any person who (1) organizes any potentially abusive tax shelter, or (2) sells any interest in such a shelter" was required to maintain "a list identifying each person who was sold an interest in such shelter." 26 U.S.C. § 6112(a) (2003). Such an organizer or seller was required to make such list available for inspection to the IRS upon request. *Id.,* § 6112(c)(1) (2003). At this late date, no one has accused the Carpenter-affiliated welfare benefit plan of having a 2:1 tax write-off ratio necessary to be an "abusive" tax shelter, and the Government has yet to establish that any of the Carpenter entities fits the definition of an "organizer" or "seller" of a tax shelter under § 6112 for the "Year/Period ended December 31, 2002," the time period stated in Agent Clark's original letter and in the letters assessing the penalties. 26 U.S.C. § 6112(a) (2003); 26 C.F.R. § 301.6112-1T (A-5) (2002); 26 C.F.R. § 301.6111-1T (A-28) (2002).

Just to summarize for the benefit of the President, American Taxpayers everywhere, and for the members of Congress who voted for the AJCA before reading its thousands of pages of new law and regulations, under the AJCA amendments, the penalty for failure to maintain or provide a list under § 6112 changed from $50 per tax shelter investor with respect to a reporting failure to $10,000 per day following 20 days of noncompliance, with no maximum penalty. (Compare, 26 U.S.C. § 6708(a) (2003) with 26 U.S.C. § 6708(a)(1) (2004)). There is no dispute that those changes became effective October 23, 2004 for lists to be maintained after that date – further modified to August 3, 2007 with the change in the Regulations discussed above. Likewise, it is undisputed that the amended § 6708 effective in 2004 does not provide that the $10,000 per day penalty applies to violations of § 6112 prior to the effective date of § 6708. 26 U.S.C. § 6708 (2004). Agent Clark sent several letters in January 2006 inquiring about a list related to the activities in the calendar year 2002, before the AJCA of October 2004 or the new regulations and definitions of August 3, 2007. The various entities all responded in February of 2006 that they were not "material advisors" required to keep any list. The IRS acknowledges receipt of those responses. But then, without any warning and three and a half years later in July 2009, your author and the four entities were hit with $5 Million in fines without any due process hearing or the ability to appeal the penalties to any court.

Thus, even if your author was to be deemed in violation of IRC § 6112 for the year ending 2002, the maximum penalty under IRC § 6708 for the period "ended 2002" was $50 per tax-shelter investor. No investors; no penalty. (See Regs. §301.6708-1T Q&A-1). Now that we know how many participants and participating employers there were in 2002 that is; we could easily calculate the potential penalty precisely, if we were running an abusive tax-shelter in 2002, which, of course, we were not. However, the list required under § 6112 does not mention the words "participant" or "participating employer" or "client list" or any other of the descriptive words Agent Clark uses to defend his penalties anywhere, and none of the participants were "material advisees" of anyone involved with the welfare benefit plans. Indeed, absent express language authorizing a retroactive application of §6708 effective in 2004, imposing a $10,000 per day penalty under the post-2004 regime for a potential 2002-2003 violation amounts to a penalty by implication, a result which is never authorized as a matter of law, as well as a penalty that is expressly prohibited by the Excessive Fines, Bill of Attainder, and Ex Post Facto Clauses of the Constitution.

Mr. President, when will you be available to discuss this unconstitutional persecution of American citizens by your Administration; an Administration that is clearly itemized for the Country to see in the GAO Report dated May 11, 2011?

Please feel free to abate these arbitrary and capricious penalties at any time – if you think you can under the laws and regulations imposed by your Commissioner of the IRS and enforced by your Justice Department. These people all work for you and they are violating the laws of the United States and you swore an oath to uphold the Constitution of the United States. Mr. President, what are you waiting for?

CHAPTER FIFTEEN

THE MOST DANGEROUS MAN
IN AMERICA

The most dangerous man in America is not who you think. Sure, the President has a secret "kill list" that has been exposed and he has ordered several drone attacks that have killed innocent villagers in Pakistan, as well as not-so-innocent American citizens without due process or any trial, but no one really fears the power of the President. Certainly no one in Congress fears the President, and many Senators have lost all respect for the President; with every Sunday broadcast, they show their absolute disdain for the President. Suffice it to say, the President is not an "evil" man or even a "bad" man. He is fundamentally a good man, a good family man, and everyone should be proud to have him as a drinking buddy. But no one fears him, and most Americans genuinely like the President. He is certainly not the "most dangerous" man in America.

To the contrary, the Commissioner of the Internal Revenue Service really is feared by all, Congressman and common man alike. The title of this chapter could easily have been "American Gestapo" because only the Commissioner can order Special Agents to stand outside your house or at the end of your driveway, or in the lobby of your office at 8:00 in the morning to serve you with a summons. The Commissioner has still not read the Second Circuit's decision in the *Schulz* case of 2005 that stated that: "No consequence whatever can befall a taxpayer who refuses, ignores, or otherwise does not comply with an IRS summons until that summons is backed by a federal court order."

Instead, the Commissioner has Special Agents threatening innocent accountants and attorneys that, if their clients do not fly across the country to answer an IRS summons, they will be jailed or fined. This is happening in 2012. IRS Special Agents interview teenage daughters for hours at a time and say: "You know your Dad is a liar and a tax cheat don't you?" If the IRS could ignore the entire Bill of Rights, they would. The Commissioner and his henchman can order the storming of a house like they did to Denise Simon or the commando raid on a small company like they did with the Charter Oak Trust. The President would not and could not do anything like that without facing impeachment.

But the Commissioner of the IRS works for the President. The President has done nothing to end this unconstitutional abuse of American citizens that pervades the American market and American economy. You don't believe that? Send an email to your attorney. Ask him or her about anything: your will, your trust, your real estate.

And, if you work with a large law firm, at the bottom of each email you receive it will say:

"To ensure compliance with requirements imposed by the IRS, we inform you that any U.S. Federal tax advice contained in this communication (including any attachments) is not intended or written to be used, and cannot be used, for the purpose of (i) avoiding penalties under the Internal Revenue Code or (ii) promoting, marketing or recommending to another party any transaction or matter addressed herein."

This is a typical "Circular 230" warning that you will find at the bottom of a typical law firm or accounting firm email. You were only asking about the closing on your house, but Circular 230 warnings are all over your attorney's email. Might as well be Circular 666 for the Apocalyptic readers out there.

This book is meant to be a continuation of Thomas Paine's "*The American Crisis*", and is written in the same spirit, but his notions of "tyranny" and "Hell" cannot possibly describe the Britain of today or the Royal Family that is loved in this country and abroad. To mention the word "Gestapo" is too inflammatory and hurts the families that suffered so much and lost family members during the Holocaust.

For example, Maine Governor Paul LePage set off a political firestorm – as well as an excellent example of Godwin's Law – by comparing the President's desire to hire 16,000 new IRS Special Agents to enforce his "Affordable Care Act" as the "New Gestapo." Certainly Governor LePage is not the first American – or even the first Republican – to compare the IRS to the dreaded Gestapo, but then again, perhaps the Democrats who are criticizing Governor LePage have not had their homes or offices raided by the IRS. Once that happens, maybe they will not be so quick to criticize the Governor's choice of analogies.

Somewhere between the hatred of British taxes and Parliamentary regulations of 1776, and the absolute horror and terror of Hitler's Nazis lies the American IRS, which must be dismantled and cut in half by the next President.

But instead, the President wants to add 16,000 Special Agents, 4,000 to hassle the rich and 12,000 to go after everyone else to make sure that they buy health insurance or pay penalties under his program. No concept of Thomas Paine's "Hell" could match the new America with IRS Special Agents monitoring your healthcare and the purchase of health insurance. For three years, I have been fighting $5,000,000 in unconstitutional penalties assessed by an IRS

Agent for the "crime" of putting life insurance in a welfare benefit plan. Millions of dollars have been wasted by the Government in attacking and abusing our Constitutional rights. If you are upset about a Congressman or a Supreme Court justice coming between you and your doctor, just wait until you "disobey" an order from an IRS "Special Agent" – the same kind the President wants to hire 16,000 more of – regarding your new "healthcare tax."

An accountant that I know in Connecticut had to hire an attorney to defend him against an IRS Special Agent from Chicago, Illinois, who actually told the Attorney in Connecticut that if the Accountant in Connecticut did not **come to Illinois** to be interviewed by the Chicago Special Agent, then the Chicago Special Agent could have the Accountant **arrested** on the Special Agent's say-so alone. This is the President's IRS and Eric Holder's Justice Department. We will see how quickly the President and the Attorney General investigate this claim of a clearly out-of-control Special Agent.

If you vote for the President, you will be supporting the most dangerous man in America, and America will become a terrorist state where the IRS can invade your home or office at any time and under the guise of the IRS's unlimited investigative powers and a sealed search warrant; go through your wife's underwear drawer or take your private papers from your office. If you do not believe that the IRS does this every day, then you must be asleep. Just Google "IRS raids" or "Government raids."

The late Democratic Senator Daniel Moynihan heard about these IRS raids during the Roth Hearings and said, "We must stop these armed commando raids on American citizens." That was in 1998. Since then, there have been the Walker Commission, the Roth Hearings, and the IRS Restructuring and Reform Act of 1998.

Yet under the President, there have been more of these illegal IRS investigative raids than at any time in U.S. history.

Take, for example, a recent trial in Boston, Massachusetts; the cradle of the American Revolution. That trial involved a property dispute between a dozen parties, and only tangentially involved a potential IRS lien on just one of the dozen parties. The IRS wanted to claim the entire property because one party had a disputed tax lien and a disputed claim to the property at the center of the action. The 45 potential jurors were asked if they ever had a problem with the IRS or had a tax lien on their property. Of the 45 jurors asked, 41 said that they had a tax lien on them at one time or another or had a tax penalty or had some tax problem with the IRS in the past.

At no time leading up to, during, or even after the American Revolution did 90% of the Colonists have a problem with King George III or Parliament. Ninety percent of Americans hate and/or fear the IRS. That makes the Commissioner of the IRS the Most Dangerous Man in America. He must be stopped. He must be replaced by the next President, and the IRS must be cut in half. Someone must be put in charge to put the word "Service" back into the IRS's name. Not only will Americans be less free and less secure in their papers and privacy with the 16,000 new Special Agents the President wants to hire, but America cannot afford to **pay** for the salary and benefits of new tax collectors, new taxes, and new regulations.

The Tax Code is six volumes, **each volume larger** than the King James Bible. One volume is the Tax Code itself which Congress creates. But the five other volumes of the Regulations all belong to the Commissioner. Without changing the Commissioner, no tax reform is possible. If the Commissioner was replaced with a visionary person like the Author, then no "tax reform" would be necessary. Smart and efficient changes could be made in the collection of taxes and implemented without waiting for Congress to act. If the Commissioner was replaced with someone who really "experienced" the Tax Code, who really "understood" the Tax Code, and someone who was committed to making the IRS a true "service" organization, then we would see the IRS as it was meant to be and not a modern day Gestapo; just as no one "fears" or "hates" the U.S. Postal Service.

It is significant to point out that Treasury Inspector General J. Russell George has criticized the IRS for sending out more than Six Billion Dollars in fraudulent tax refunds, whereas the current deficit for the Post Office is only about Five Billion Dollars. Instead of calling for the privatization of the U.S. Postal Service, someone in Washington should just propose that we end Saturday delivery, terminate a lot of unnecessary employees, transform pension plans into defined contribution voluntary 401(k) plans, and end post-retirement health benefits for retired postal workers that nobody else in America has. At the same time, the Commissioner of the IRS should be fired and replaced immediately for his negligence in this area, and the savings of replacing the Commissioner would end the fraud and the waste that is costing the American taxpayers between Six Billion and 21 Billion Dollars, which can be used to take care of not only the Post Office deficit, but uninsured emergency room visits, and pay off some delinquent student loan indebtedness for gradu- ates in nursing and with medical degrees, who decide to work in free healthcare clinics for the poor for a period of two to four years.

Let us all work to make America a better place to live and work, and the IRS as dependable as the U.S. Postal Service. We must replace the Commissioner and the President. There is no other way.

CHAPTER SIXTEEN
A GOVERNMENT OF COWARDS

Attorney General Eric Holder made a famous speech that is on the Government's and the USDOJ's websites, where he stated the following:

> One cannot truly understand America without understanding the historical experience of black people in this nation. Simply put, to get to the heart of this country one must examine its racial soul. Though this nation has proudly thought of itself as an ethnic melting pot, in things racial we have always been and continue to be, in too many ways, essentially a nation of cowards. Though race related issues continue to occupy a significant portion of our political discussion, and though there remain many unresolved racial issues in this nation, we, average Americans, simply do not talk enough with each other about race. But we must do more- and we in this room bear a special responsibility. Through its work and through its example this Department of Justice, as long as I am here, must - and will - lead the nation to the "new birth of freedom" so long ago promised by our greatest President. This is our duty and our solemn obligation.
>
> http://www.justice.gov/ag/speeches/2009/ag-speech-090218.html

But this is the same Attorney General that is the boss of the cesspool of jurisprudence known as the Boston U.S. Attorney's Office. If you read the USA Today study done on egregious prosecutorial misconduct – see USA Today, "Prosecutors'

Conduct Can Tip Justice Scales," Sept. 23, 2010 – you will see that prosecutorial misconduct is rampant across the country and the worst U.S. Attorney's office in the United States according to the study is the U.S. Attorney's office in Boston. Notice that this is called the "Nation of Cowards" speech, and **not** the "New Birth of Freedom" speech.

If you are Black, and you care about your fellow brother, then you cannot in good conscience vote for the President because you will just prolong the political hypocrisy of Attorney General Holder and the President. Google Darwin Jones and Judge Wolf. Read Judge Wolf's 60-page opinion excoriating the AUSA prosecutor Suzanne Sullivan. Judge Wolf reported the entire U.S. Attorney's office to the Office of Professional Responsibility (OPR) and sent several letters to Attorney General Eric Holder himself. Note that the Darwin Jones case starts as a young black man "on a bicycle." As is typical in Boston, Federal prosecutors want to take young black men off the streets – and off their bicycles – and punish them under Federal laws meant for mobsters and drug kingpins so that a teenager with a gun receives a mandatory 10 year sentence. If you add just an ounce of cocaine (28 grams to an ounce) then you have another minimum 10 year sentence added to that. Take for example the recent case of Rodney "Righteous" Gurley, who made the New York Times because Judge Young (former Chief Judge in Massachusetts) had the courage to defy the prosecutors who sought to try Gurley in Federal court to get the minimum 10 year sentence. When Judge Young put the question to the jury and the jury came back with the wrong answer that Gurley did not possess the minimum amount of cocaine necessary for a mandatory 10 year sentence, Judge Young gave Gurley a three year sentence, which the Government is appealing. Note, however, that Gurley was already facing life without parole in Massachusetts state court for being suspected of being involved with the killing of the man who really did murder his brother, Jose Gurley.

Attorney General Holder is doing nothing to protect the rights or improve the lives of young black men in Boston, and if not for the courage of Chief Judge Mark Wolf and former Chief Judge Young to report the incredible abuses of the prosecutors in their voluminous opinions that are published all over the country, no one would be aware of the rampant prosecutorial misconduct against young Black and Hispanic men being carried out by the President's Justice Department in cities like Boston. Instead of the President or Eric Holder investigating the prosecution of innocent black men, they would rather ignore Judge Wolf and allow innocent black men to be put to death, like Troy Davis. Several young people in our office were wearing "I am Troy Davis" shirts after he was put to death, despite the fact that <u>seven</u> witnesses recanted their testimony and said he was not even there when the police officer was shot. The President could have easily commuted the death sentence to life in prison, while the Attorney General granted a Federal investigation into Troy Davis' claims of innocence and the possible perjury of witnesses. Why not do that? Because the President and Eric Holder are political cowards that would rather see young black men put in prison or put to death than to look weak in front of "conservative" white voters.

What about granting a pardon for Shane Matthews? Ten years for having two "bricks" of marijuana? Why not commute Troy Davis' death sentence to life in prison after seven witnesses recanted their testimony and some of the witnesses admitted to outright lies? Compare that to the Alford Plea accepted in the West Memphis Three case in Arkansas and Haley Barbour's 100 pardons in Mississippi. In the West Memphis Three case, even the parents of the murdered children believe that they were innocent and Damien Echols was on death row for 18 years, just as Troy Davis was. Who better to commute Troy Davis' death sentence than a Black Attorney General and a Black President? But you do not want to interfere in the business of the States? That has not stopped either

Attorney General Holder or the President from interfering in the business of all 50 states, whether it be Arizona's borders, Alaska's oil, or the enforcement of the President's "Affordable Care Act" by 16,000 new IRS Special Agents.

However, the worst case of prosecutorial misconduct in the Boston U.S. Attorney's office was committed by Prosecutor Jon Mitchell, who is an Eliot Spitzer wannabe. Mitchell put a young black man in prison claiming he was a big drug dealer and ran his whole campaign for Mayor based on that one prosecution. Google Shane Matthews on YouTube and see his video and his song about two bricks of marijuana. He could have been on "American Idol" or "America's Got Talent," but instead he is serving 10 years in a Federal jail at your expense. The citizens of New Bedford, Massachusetts even believed Mitchell's hogwash about putting a "dangerous" drug dealer behind bars and then elected him as their new Mayor.

"Mayor" Mitchell now claims on his website that he brought down the infamous Whitey Bulger, who eluded Boston authorities for all of those years despite the fact that his brother was the President of the University of Massachusetts and Whitey made frequent trips to Mexico for his prescription drugs. If Jon Mitchell were ever in the same room with Whitey Bulger, Mitchell would faint after soiling his pants. For the benefit of the citizens of New Bedford, let me make the following points:

Prosecutor Mitchell is the most dangerous form of liar. He can lie so smoothly and convincingly for his own gain that it is difficult to believe he is not telling the truth. Believe me, he is lying about two things that concern you. First, that he cares about New Bedford, and second, that he was a good Prosecutor.

Prosecutor Mitchell is also the worst form of civil servant – he is charming, charismatic, well-educated, went to Harvard, so he feels it is his God-given entitlement to run for Mayor, then Congressman, then Governor and eventually President. Much like Eliot Spitzer, he really doesn't care about you – the citizens – your graduation rate, the schools, the joblessness of your young people, the litter in the streets, and the care and protection of your senior citizens. He only cares about himself and the next political stepping stone he will seek when it opens.

But Prosecutor Mitchell's only claim to fame on his own website is that he put a drug dealer away under the Federal laws for ten years. That drug dealer was no Whitey Bulger. That young man was someone's son, brother, nephew, cousin. He was turned in by his ex-girlfriend. It costs you $48,000 a year - $500,000 to put him in a cage for 10 years – better to send him to Harvard for four years like Prosecutor Mitchell. The prosecution probably cost another $500,000, and the young man eventually pled guilty after his homemade video was shown in Court with him singing about $10,000 of marijuana. Do you feel safer that Prosecutor Mitchell got this young man off the streets?

Prosecutor Mitchell cost you citizens $500,000 in the prosecution of a young man that did nothing more than smoke the same things the President did while he was at Harvard; and then another $500,000 to keep him locked up in a cage at taxpayers' expense for the next 10 years – never to find gainful employment the rest of his life because he is an ex-con – so that will cost you more money down the road in welfare, unemployment, and food stamps. What happened to the old days when a young man got into trouble and the judge and the prosecutor would get together and offer the accused the chance of going to jail or serving in the Army? That same young man could have been an Airborne Ranger, or a Navy Seal, had Prosecutor Mitchell given him the chance to serve his country and not put him away at your expense.

But what about the not so successful cases? Attorney Mitchell does not advertise that two planes involved in the 9-11 tragedy took off from Logan Airport. He and then U.S. Attorney Michael Sullivan spent tens of Millions of dollars and did not find a single terrorist to prosecute. Only Shane Matthews, because of his ex-girlfriend and his YouTube video that was played for the jury.

And how about the way Mitchell and his fellow prosecutors handled the case of Vincent "the Animal" Ferrara, who admittedly had several people killed as the leader of the Boston Mafia, but was released from prison anyway due to the egregious prosecutorial misconduct of the Government prosecutors who first tried to frame him for the murder of his best friend, and then tried to hide all of the evidence that showed he was innocent of that crime? See <u>Boston Globe</u>, "Ex-Mob Leader Freed from Prison," May 27, 2005. When you read Judge Wolf's opinions of the U.S. Attorney's office in Boston, you will see they had to pay over $100,000,000 to the families of known mobsters because of the job Prosecutor Mitchell and his cronies did. This is $100,000,000 of taxpayer money in wrongful damages done to mobster families.

Then there is the case of Bernie Madoff. Harry Markopolos writes in his book, "<u>No One Would Listen</u>," that he brought the

Madoff case to the **Feds in Boston** on a silver platter, not once but three times from 2002-2005. Why didn't Attorney Mitchell and U.S. Attorney Sullivan go after Madoff in 2004 and 2005?

Prosecutor Mitchell could have saved the Madoff clients BILLIONS if he had only listened to Harry Markopolos. Massachusetts' clients of Madoff lost over $8 Billion in the Madoff fraud. He was probably too busy accepting the guilty plea from that dangerous rapper from New Bedford, who was turned in by his ex-girlfriend. Don't you feel safer now knowing how Prosecutor Mitchell is looking out for you and your family in New Bedford?

Essentially the job of Mayor is to make sure the potholes get fixed, the stoplights work, the streets get plowed in the winter, and the school buses run on time. You had two wonderful candidates, Tony Cabral and Linda Morad that clearly loved your city and were willing to do the tough work that needs to be done to make sure everything works. They wanted to become Mayor to be true civil servants – to literally work for you and serve your families. They felt a need – a duty – to serve their fellow man through service to the community. Look at their websites and their careers and what people say about them.

Not so with Prosecutor Mitchell. He doesn't care about you – the city – or even the potholes or the school buses. He is just a younger version of Eliot Spitzer. His entire career was spent putting Black and Hispanic youths behind bars. Even Judge Wolf – the Chief Judge in Boston – accused Prosecutors like Mitchell and Sullivan of turning the Federal Courthouse into a municipal court with petty drug and gun violations just so they could put people away for 10 years instead of 90 days in state court. Just Google **"Sullivan is an unethical prosecutor"** and see what comes up. Prosecutor Mitchell is 100 times worse than Prosecutor Sullivan ever was. Prosecutor Mitchell suborned perjury in several cases, and will probably be disbarred within the next three years.

Please remember that New Bedford has a noble heritage and history. It was the home of Frederick Douglass and other great abolitionist leaders. Frederick Douglass lived, fought, and died to make all men free and to end the evil of slavery. Now he must be spinning in his grave that Prosecutor Mitchell, who has made his career putting young black men in jail – as if that is a noble accomplishment – is the Mayor of the City that Frederick Douglass called home.

New Bedford was once famous for welcoming new immigrants to the New World – America – whether they be Portuguese, Irish, or even from the Azores. But now Prosecutor Mitchell wants to raid innocent local businesses and deport hundreds of so-called "illegal" immigrants who just wanted a better life for their families. Is that who you really want to be your Mayor? Start the recall process now.

Prosecutor Mitchell doesn't care about you, your city, or your problems. He cares about just one thing: his beautiful career. It is up to you fine people of this great city to harpoon the whale before it is too late. The famous New Bedford Whaling motto says it best: "A dead whale or a stove boat!"

Prosecutor Mitchell's illustrious political career is the "whale" and New Bedford is the boat. You have the power to stop Prosecutor Mitchell's political career – right here – right now. Start the recall process. Vote him out of office, for your families and for your children's future. Great job Prosecutor Mitchell is doing with the school system, right? The crime rate is <u>up</u>, not down under Prosecutor Mitchell. No ex-girlfriends to turn in cold-blooded killers. No YouTube video to play for the jury. Make Prosecutor Mitchell get a real job in this terrible economy, made even worse by bureaucrats like him in Washington, D.C.

According to the statistics compiled by CityRating.com, the crime rate for 2012 is on track and expected to be higher than New Bedford's previous worst year of 2009. In 2009, the New Bedford crime rate was 197% higher than the national average for violent crimes, and was 179% higher than the average violent crime rate for Massachusetts per CityRating.com.

Since Prosecutor Mitchell took office in January 2012, the entire year belongs to his Administration, but in many categories of crime, the number of crimes as of July 2012 already surpassed the 2009 level, and by December of 2012, it is projected the year 2012 will be New Bedford's worst year ever for violent crimes with as many 4,500 projected crimes by year end. To his credit, however, Mayor Mitchell did have his old friends in the Boston U.S. Attorney's Office round up 44 more young Hispanic men, known as the Latin Kings, for random drug crimes – meaning they sold drugs to under-cover agents working for the Federal government in New Bedford. This is at the same time that there is a crisis at the New Bedford School System, a lack of leadership in the Harbor Development Commission, massive layoffs by local companies, and thanks to Mayor Mitchell, New Bedford will experience a huge economic loss next year – as much as $80 Million – due to new fishing regulations that will destroy the fishing industry in New Bedford.

You voted for this guy because he is "famous" for getting "dangerous" drug dealers like Shane Matthews of YouTube fame off the streets of New Bedford. Yet New Bedford, under the Prosecutor Mitchell Administration, is slated to become the most violent city in Massachusetts as its historic fishing industry is decimated. Please Google "Crime is up in New Bedford thanks to Mayor Mitchell," and just read the stories for yourself. As a famous philosopher once said: "Every nation (city) has the government it deserves." You made a mistake, you were lied to, you deserve better.

You know what he will probably do if he is no longer Mayor? He will get a job with a big, fancy, overpriced law firm in Boston where he will charge $800 an hour to defend the same drug dealers he was "famous" for putting away. He will say "Pay my fee" or you will go away for 10 years like the "video rap artist" Shane Matthews. Prosecutor Mitchell will now become "prostitute" Mitchell and sell his "legal" services to the highest bidder. And who might that be? The only people that will trust their personal freedom and liberty to the likes of ex- Prosecutor Mitchell will be the same drug dealers he wants you to believe are a threat to your community now. There are way too many young Black and Hispanic kids in prison in America, and that is because of unethical prosecutors like Prosecutor Mitchell. Just ask the great jurists like Judge Wolf and

Judge Young who are doing more to protect young black men and Hispanic youth than Mayor Mitchell, Attorney General Holder, and the President combined.

Prosecutor Mitchell does not care one bit about your schools, the high drop-out rate, the high unemployment rate, or the total lack of jobs for the young people of New Bedford. Prosecutor Mitchell is a bureaucrat. He does not know how to create jobs, he only knows how to bust people that give jobs to "illegal" aliens and to put young Black and Hispanic people behind bars for 10 years for "dealing" a different brand of tobacco than the local liquor store sells, but the same brand the President once smoked.

Let me close this chapter with a personal message to Prosecutor Mitchell that is inscribed on the walls of the Moakley Courthouse that Judge Wolf and Judge Young go by every day on the way to their chambers, just waiting to experience the egregious prosecutorial misconduct of Prosecutor Mitchell that you can read about in the famous USA Today study on prosecutorial misconduct (see USA Today, "Prosecutors' Conduct Can Tip Justice Scales," Sept. 23, 2010) that named the District of Massachusetts the worst U.S. Attorney's Office in the country for prosecutorial misconduct:

"Our Government is the potent, the omnipresent teacher. For good or for ill, it teaches the whole people by its example. Crime is contagious. If the Government becomes a lawbreaker, it breeds contempt for law; it invites every man to become a law unto himself; it invites anarchy. To declare that, in the administration of the criminal law, the end justifies the means – **to declare that the Government may commit crimes in order to secure the conviction of a private citizen – would bring terrible retribution. Against that pernicious doctrine this Court should resolutely set its face.**" *Olmstead v. United States,* 277 U.S. 428 (1928) (emphasis added).

Citizens of New Bedford, do yourselves a favor, protect your family's future and your own, and start the recall vote now for Prosecutor Mitchell to get a new job other than as your Mayor. Once you know the real truth, you will believe that Prosecutor Mitchell is not fit to clean the streets of your fair city with a broom, much less be Mayor.

CHAPTER SEVENTEEN
AN OPEN LETTER TO EDUARDO SAVERIN

Now that you have surpassed Bradley Manning and Julian Assange of WikiLeaks fame on the list of greatest American traitors because of your decision to relocate to Singapore and give up your American citizenship and passport, it was time for someone to come to your defense. Rest easy that you are still way behind Benedict Arnold in the standings, but you should know that no Democratic Senators ever tried to illegally seize any of Benedict Arnold's property, or even Julius and Ethel Rosenberg's property. It is embarrassing that Senators who swore an oath to uphold the Constitution "against all enemies, foreign and domestic" either never read the Constitution or do not understand what the prohibitions against "ex post facto" laws or "bills of attainder" really mean. They should reread the chapter of this book entitled "The Section 6708 Affair." In any event, someone in America should speak up in your defense.

First, Singapore is the freest nation on Earth. If you do not believe that, just Google "Index of Economic Freedom for 2012" or ask famous "investment-biker" Jim Rogers. If you believe that Hong Kong in China is really number one, then there is nothing that can be done to help you. Hong Kong is not really a country, and its people are controlled by Communist China and its policies. America should be number one on the list, but it has had a tough time making the top ten. And no one seems to care that America is ranked number 17 in Reading, number 23 in Science, and number 31 in Mathematics on the list of countries in the rankings for student test scores in the 2009 Programme for International Student Assessment (PISA); whereas Singapore, ranked number 5 in Reading, number 4 in Science, number 2 in Mathematics, is always near the top of the list in **<u>every</u>** popular listing.

Second, like all of the Facebook founders, you will not be paying any income taxes or estate taxes on your newfound wealth. You do not need to go to Singapore to save on capital gains taxes; you just need to set up a Charitable Remainder Trust like Jim Cramer did – and which he mentions six times a night on his famous television show, but never really explains what a Charitable Remainder Trust is. While recommending and panning stocks to his faithful listeners, he never once explains to his fans that he pays **<u>no taxes</u>** on his eight figure wealth because all of his investments are in a Charitable Remainder Trust. So, he pays no taxes on interest, does not care that the tax on dividends will go from 15% to 40% beginning January 1, 2013, and he has enjoyed a **<u>permanent</u>** reduction on his capital gains taxes since he discovered the beauty of the Charitable Remainder Trust. Of course all of the wealthy people in Silicon Valley have Charitable Remainder Trusts. Even the Democratic Senators that accused you of tax evasion have Charitable Remainder Trusts. Only the poor and the middle class taxpayers do not have Charitable Remainder Trusts. Additionally, all of the Facebook Founders set up Grantor Retained Annuity Trusts (GRATs) – just like all the Walton heirs did so they could legally escape Federal Estate and Gift Taxes like all of the wealthy people in America do. And the venerable Tax Court even approved that totally bogus device to escape Estate Taxes and Gift Taxes. No one in the Senate complained about that. If Sam Walton's heirs do not need to pay Estate Taxes (and neither will Governor Romney's heirs), then why should you?

Third, everyone knows that Singapore is the best nation to start new businesses. Easy to set up new companies and take them public. No Sarbanes-Oxley – no Dodd-Frank – no one goes to jail for making misstatements on a filing statement or a financial form. Your fear, and rightfully so, was that certain investment bankers at Morgan Stanley might make material misrepresentations on all the paperwork that was used to take Facebook public. You knew that the Facebook IPO was one big fraud on the public from the get-go, and that once those Democratic Senators that accused you of "tax evasion" over a mere $300 Million realized that Facebook insiders, investment bankers, and certain hedge funds actually defrauded

American investors to the tune of FIFTY BILLION DOLLARS or more, you did not want to be there when the Congressional hearings started. You were the person who started Facebook. If not for your cash investment in the beginning, Facebook would not exist today, and the Winkelvoss Twins probably would have won in court. You made it into Harvard on your own, and Zuckerberg needed you and your family connections and money – not vice versa. Computer programmers are a dime a dozen. You realized the value of the idea. The next good idea that comes along – you will have the "gold" and you will make the "rules," not someone else; and certainly not Sean Parker.

If Congress grilled Jamie Dimon over his London office losing a mere Two Billion Dollars of JPMorgan Chase's own money, what will Congress do when they learn that Morgan Stanley and the Facebook Gang defrauded American investors of over FIFTY BILLION DOLLARS? Forget the fact that Morgan Stanley let their favorite and best clients know that all the Facebook numbers were fluffed up – and that they lifted the price from $28 a share to $38 a share and increased the number of shares available for insiders to sell. Forget all that. The real crime was letting their Hedge Fund clients get access to shares – not to buy – but to sell short. If the Facebook public offering was not a massive securities fraud, you might as well close down the SEC right now. Morgan Stanley literally made it possible for their big Hedge Fund clients to "steal" FIFTY BILLION DOLLARS from the gullible American public. The Sir Allen Stamford fraud was only SEVEN BILLION DOLLARS and the Bernie Madoff fraud was actually only TWELVE BILLION DOLLARS in real money terms, but the Facebook fraud will be the greatest fraud of all time. After the FIFTY BILLION DOLLAR Facebook fraud, everyone should realize the stock market game is rigged against the typical American investor by the Wall Street bankers. However, just like with the 2008 debacle, no one will go to jail for this one either.

Fourth, if you sold all or most of your Facebook holdings during The Public Offering (good title for follow-up movie by the people who did The Social Network), then you have Three Billion Dollars to invest. By being in Singapore, you have access to China (the soon to be largest GDP nation on Earth), and the Hong Kong, Shanghai, and Australian stock markets as well as the Singapore stock market. All of the best ideas will come to you, all of the smart young techies overseas will come to you, and you can become the "Warren Buffett" of a new, free, and up-and-coming nation. In America, the courts do not protect you; they only try to put you in jail. Singapore gets a little piece of all the trade between Brazil and China, and those Democratic Senators that wanted to demonize you do not realize that America has lost its trade position with China to Brazil, and because of your Brazilian birth, you speak the language and because of your Harvard education, you are the best person in the World to set up new companies to trade between Brazil and China. Australia is already a "colony" of China – not just a trade partner, but Singapore is closer to China and better situated. Had you defected to English-speaking Australia or Bermuda, would anyone have cared? Maybe, if they were ignorant enough to think that you are leaving for "tax-evasion" purposes. Most Americans believe Singapore is a backwards, Third-World nation, without running water, flushing toilets, or even the right kind of toilet paper. Remember England in the early 1970's? Oh, you were not even born then.

Fifth, you are also smart enough to realize that as of April 2012, the United States has the **highest corporate tax** in the World. Singapore has a flat tax of 8.5% for small companies and 17% for those companies making more than $300,000. But more importantly, Singapore has a **zero-percent** dividends tax on distributions to shareholders and **zero-percent** capital gains tax. It also has (since 2008) a **zero-percent** estate tax. But, if you become the Warren Buffett of Singapore, you can set up a new holding company in

Singapore (in a few hours or less) and invest in only U.S.-based companies. Singapore does not tax earnings from outside of Singapore. So your new holding company, Hathaway-Berkshire International (HBI), only invests in American dividend-paying companies. Your Singapore Holding Company HBI pays no taxes on the money received from foreign sources. Any sales of stock are not taxed. Borrowing from your stock holdings does not create taxable income (even here), and when you make distributions to yourself as dividends from your company, it is not taxable. So, if you invested your Three Billion of Facebook profits in American companies in the U.S., you would face double taxation – once at the corporate level and a second time at the personal level. In Singapore, your holding company could invest in American REITs and MLPs and pay no taxes at all in Singapore. If you assume that you made only 10% per year on your Three Billion; that would mean that you save $120,000,000 in U.S. taxes each and every year based on your $300,000,000 of income from American companies. You are such a young man, but even at his attained age, Warren Buffett would probably move from Omaha to Singapore to save $120 Million a year in American taxes, and he would probably take his now famous Secretary along with the entire Netjets operation to avoid that amount of annual taxes.

Sixth, but that is not the real reason that you are leaving. You only came to the United States because your parents discovered that you were on a list of potential kidnapping targets in Brazil, and former Brazilian president Fernando Collor had frozen all saving accounts making doing business in Brazil a nightmare. Once you came to Miami to be safe from the kidnappers, you were a good student and you got into Harvard on your own. You actually beat a famous Grandmaster in chess at age 13. In contrast, the overall crime rate in Singapore is one tenth that of most American cities – and violent crimes, because of the civilized British nature and culture – are almost non-existent in comparison to American cities.

Seventh, Operation FATCAT – the newly adopted Foreign Account Tax Compliance Act, basically prevents American citizens from opening bank accounts overseas – or even doing business abroad. No foreign banks want to have American clients anymore because of the compliance paperwork required by the IRS. Only well-to-do businessmen and entrepreneurs need foreign bank accounts. Drug dealers and tax evaders already know how to launder their money without using Swiss Bank accounts, and even Governor Romney has an account in the Caymans. No one has accused Governor Romney of being a drug dealer, tax evader, or American traitor. Even if you wanted to be loyal to your adopted

America, it was Operation FATCAT that required you to leave, and none of the Democratic Senators even mentioned that new legislation and IRS regulations.

Eighth, the Sun always shines in Singapore. Not only is the weather always great in Singapore; the trains and the streets really are cleaner than in America; the beaches and surrounding islands are beautiful; the restaurants, hotels, and nightlife are world-renowned; and Singapore is the **only** city-nation-state in the World to have not just one, but two airline terminals in the Top-Ten. And no less a business expert than <u>Forbes</u> lists Singapore at the top of the "Easiest Places to do Business" list as well as the "Best Places to do Business" list, and just behind Qatar for highest per capita wealth. World travelers, business people and tourists alike list Singapore at the top in almost every category. Just like international tennis stars used to leave their high-taxed nations for Monte Carlo, you are smart enough to realize that Singapore is the new Monte Carlo for a world that is no longer Euro-centric. You have been living there since 2009, so the real reason you are giving up your American citizenship is not to save on any taxes, but to avoid Operation FATCAT making all the banks in Singapore throw you out simply because they do not want to comply with new regulations enforced by America's IRS.

The Democratic Senators would rather demonize you rather than say "How did we lose out to Singapore in all of the standings that count: Freedom, Privacy, Taxation, Ease of Doing Business, Lack of Regulation, Math, Science, Technology, Infrastructure, Hotel Service, Transportation, and Lifestyle?" You realize that Singapore beats us in each of those important categories, and no one has talked about the low unemployment rate and the booming economy. There are no IRS raids in Singapore. Singapore has grown its national per capita wealth in the past ten years, not seen it cut in half to 1991 levels as we have had here in America.

We used to be Singapore – number one in every category that counts – and sadly we are not anymore. While it is easy to criticize you for leaving your adopted country, the truth is that we all need to work harder to make you **want** to come back. The Democratic Senators do not get it. God bless you for being a good person, a great American entrepreneur, and for bringing this sad state of affairs to our attention.

THE GRYPHON
PRESIDENCY

CHAPTER EIGHTEEN
THE GRYPHON
ACCEPTANCE SPEECH

America's rise to world leadership in the past century has reflected more than anything else our unprecedented economic growth. Interrupted during the decade of the 30s, the vigorous expansion of our economy resumed in 1940 and continued thereafter. It demonstrated for all to see the power of freedom and the efficiency of free institutions. The economic health of this nation has been, up until now, fundamentally sound.

But a leading nation, a nation upon which all depend, not only in this country but around the World, cannot afford to be satisfied, to look back, or to pause. Our strength and growth depends on the strength of others, the spread of free world trade and unity, and continued confidence in our leadership and our currency. The underdeveloped countries are dependent upon us for the sale of their primary commodities and for aid to their struggling economies. In short, a prosperous and growing America is important not only to Americans, it is — as the spokesman for the Western nations in the Organization for Economic Cooperation and Development, — of vital importance to the entire World.

This economy is capable of producing, without strain, much more than we are producing today. Business earnings could be seven to eight times higher than they are today. Utilization of existing plant and equipment could be much higher — and, if it were, investment would rise. We need not accept an unemployment rate of nine percent or more, such as we have had for the last 36 months. There is no need for us to be satisfied with a rate of growth that keeps good men out of work and good capacity out of use.

We are all, of course, familiar with these problems. The rate of insured unemployment has been persistently higher here than the national average, and the increases in personal income and employment have been slower here than in the nation as a whole. You have seen the tragedy of chronically depressed areas, of unemployed young people — and I think this might be one of our most serious national problems, unemployed young people, those under 20. One out of four are unemployed — particularly those in the minority groups, roaming the streets of our great cities — and others on relief at an early age, with the prospect that in this decade we will have between seven and eight Million school dropouts, unskilled, coming into the labor market, at a time when the need for unskilled labor is steadily diminishing. And we know you share our conviction that this nation's economy can and must do better than it has done in the last five years. Our choice, therefore, boils down to one of: doing nothing, and thereby risking a widening gap between our actual and potential growth in output, profits, and employment

— or taking action, at the federal level, to raise our entire economy to a new and higher level of business activity.

If we do not take action, those who have the most reason to be dissatisfied with our present rate of growth will be tempted to seek shortsighted and narrow solutions — to resist automation, to reduce the work week to 35 hours or even lower, to shut out imports, or to raise prices in a vain effort to obtain full capacity profits on under-capacity operations. But these are all self-defeating expedients which can only restrict the economy, not expand it.

There are a number of ways by which the Federal government can meet its responsibilities to aid economic growth. It can and must improve American education and technical training. It can and must expand civilian research and technology. One of the great bottlenecks for this country's economic growth in this decade will be the shortages of doctorates in mathematics, engineering, and physics — a serious shortage with a great demand and an undersupply of highly trained manpower. We can and must step up the development of our natural resources.

But the most direct and significant kind of federal action aiding economic growth is to make possible an increase in private consumption and investment demand — to cut the fetters which hold back private spending. In the past, this could be done in part by the increased use of credit and monetary tools, but our balance of payments situation today places limits on our use of those tools for expansion. It could also be done by increasing federal expenditures more rapidly than necessary, but such a course would soon demoralize both the government and our economy. If government is to retain the confidence of the people, it must not spend more than can be justified on grounds of national need or spent with maximum efficiency. And we shall say more on this in a moment.

The final and best means of strengthening demand among consumers and business is to reduce the burden on private income and the deterrents to private initiative which are imposed by our present tax system.

We are not talking about a "quickie" or a temporary tax cut, which would be more appropriate if a recession were imminent. Nor are we talking about giving the economy a mere shot in the arm, to ease some temporary complaint. We are talking about the accumulated evidence of the last five years that our present tax system, developed as it was, in good part, during World War II to restrain growth, exerts too heavy a drag on growth in peace time; that it siphons out of the private economy too large a share of personal and business purchasing power; that it reduces the financial incentives for personal effort, investment, and risk-taking. In short, to increase demand and lift the economy, the Federal government's most useful role is not to rush into a program of excessive increases in public expenditures, but to expand the incentives and opportunities for private expenditures.

Under these circumstances, any new tax legislation — and you can understand that under the comity which exists in the United States Constitution whereby the Ways and Means Committee in the House of Representatives have the responsibility of initiating this legislation, that the details of any proposal should wait on the meeting of the Congress in January. But you can understand that, under these circumstances, in general, that any new tax legislation enacted next year should meet the following three tests:

First, it should reduce the net taxes by a sufficiently early date and a sufficiently large amount to do the job required. Early action could give us extra leverage, added results, and important insurance against recession. Too large a tax cut, of course, could result in inflation and insufficient future revenues — but the greater danger is a tax cut too little, or too late, to be effective.

Second, the new tax bill must increase private consumption, as well as investment. Consumers are still spending between 92 and 94 percent on their after-tax income, as they have every year since 1950. But that after-tax income could and should be greater, providing stronger markets for the products of American industry. When consumers purchase more goods, plants use more of their capacity, men are hired instead of laid-off, investment increases, and profits are high.

Corporate tax rates must also be cut to increase incentives and the availability of investment capital. The government has already taken major steps to reduce business tax liability and to stimulate the modernization, replacement, and expansion of our productive plant and equipment. Now we need to increase consumer demand to make these measures fully effective — demand which will make more use of existing capacity and thus increase both profits and the incentive to invest. In fact, profits after taxes would be at least 15 percent higher today if we were operating at full employment.

For all these reasons, next year's tax legislation should reduce personal as well as corporate income taxes: for those in the lower brackets, who are certain to spend their additional take-home pay, and for those in the middle and upper brackets, who can thereby be encouraged to undertake additional efforts and enabled to invest more capital.

Third, the new tax legislation should improve both the equity and the simplicity of our present tax system. This means the enactment of long-needed tax reforms, a broadening of the tax base, and the elimination or modification of many special tax privileges. These steps are not only needed to recover lost revenue and thus make possible a larger cut in present rates, they are also tied directly to our goal of greater growth. For the present patchwork of special provisions and preferences lightens the tax loads of some only at the cost of placing a heavier burden on others. It distorts economic judgments and channels undue amounts of energy into efforts to avoid tax liability. It makes certain types of less productive activity more profitable than other more valuable undertakings. All this inhibits our growth and efficiency, as well as considerably complicating the work of both the taxpayer and the Internal Revenue Service.

These various exclusions and concessions have been justified [in the past] as a means of overcoming oppressively high rates in the upper brackets, and a sharp reduction in those rates — accompanied by base-broadening, loophole-closing measures — would properly make the new rates not only lower, but also more widely applicable. Surely this is more equitable on both counts.

Those are the three tests which the right kind of legislation must meet — and we are confident that the enactment of the right bill next year will in due course increase our gross national product by several times the amount of taxes actually cut. Profit margins will be improved, and both the incentive to invest and the supply of internal funds for investment will be increased. There will be new interest in taking risks, in increasing productivity, in creating new jobs and new products for long-term economic growth.

Other national problems, moreover, will be aided by full employment. It will encourage the location of new plants in areas of labor surplus — and provide new jobs for workers that we are retraining — and facilitate the adjustment which will be necessary under our new trade expansion bill, and reduce a number of government expenditures.

It will not, I am confident, revive an inflationary spiral or adversely affect our balance of payments. If the economy today were operating close to capacity levels with little unemployment, then we would oppose tax reductions as irresponsible and inflationary — and we would not hesitate to recommend a tax increase, if that were necessary. But our resources and manpower are not being fully utilized, the general level of prices has been remarkably stable, and increased competition — both at home and abroad — along with increased productivity, will help keep both prices and wages within appropriate limits.

The same is true of our balance of payments. While rising demand will expand imports, new investment in more efficient productive facilities will aid exports, and a new economic climate could both draw capital from abroad and keep capital here at home. It will also put us in a better position, if necessary, to use monetary tools to help our international accounts. But most importantly, confidence in the dollar in the long run rests on confidence in America, in our ability to meet our economic commitments and reach our economic goals.

But what concerns most Americans about a tax cut, I know, is not the deficit in our balance of payments but the deficit in our federal budget. Therefore, the Government should neither postpone our tax cut plans nor cut into essential national security programs.

Our true choice is not between tax reduction, on the one hand, and the avoidance of large federal deficits on the other. It is increasingly clear that no matter what party is in power, so long as our national security needs keep rising, an economy hampered by restrictive tax rates will never produce enough revenues to balance our budget — just as it will never produce enough jobs or enough profits. Surely the lesson of the last decade is that budget deficits are not caused by just wild-eyed spenders, but also by slow economic growth and periodic recessions, and any new recession would break all deficit records.

In short, it is a paradoxical truth that tax rates are too high today and tax revenues are too low and the soundest way to raise the revenues in the long run is to cut the rates now. The experiences of a number of European countries and Japan have borne this out. This country's own experience with tax reduction in the past has borne this out. And the reason is that only full employment can balance the budget, and tax reduction can pave the way to full employment. The purpose of cutting taxes now is not to incur a larger budget deficit, but to achieve the more prosperous, expanding economy which can bring about a balanced budget, and even a budget surplus. I repeat: our practical choice is not between a tax-cut deficit and a budgetary surplus. It is between two kinds of deficits: a chronic deficit of inertia, as the unwanted result of inadequate revenues and a restricted economy, or a temporary deficit of transition, resulting from a tax cut designed to boost the economy, increase tax revenues, and achieve, we believe — and we believe this can be done — a budget surplus. The first type of deficit is a sign of waste and weakness; the second reflects an investment in the future.

Nevertheless, as the Chairman of the House Ways and Means Committee pointed out, the size of the deficit is to be regarded with concern, and tax reduction must be accompanied, in his words, by "increased control of the rises in expenditures." This is precisely the course we intend to follow. This is not an easy task. During the past nine years, domestic civilian expenditures in the national government have risen at an average rate of more than seven-and-one-half percent. State and local government expenditures have risen at an annual rate of nine percent. Expenditures by the New York State government alone, for example, have risen in recent years at the rate of roughly ten percent per year. This budget will reflect, among other economies, a Billion dollar reduction in the postal deficit — and a saving[s] of Billions of dollars from the cancellation of obsolete or unworkable weapons systems. The Secretary of Defense is undertaking a cost reduction program expected to save Billions of dollars a year in the Department of Defense, cutting down on duplication and closing down nonessential installations. Other agencies must do the same.

In addition, as President, I would direct all heads of government departments and agencies to hold federal employment under the levels authorized by Congressional appropriations, to absorb through greater efficiency a substantial part of this year's federal pay increase, to achieve an increase in productivity which will enable the same amount of work to be done by less people, and to refrain from spending any unnecessary funds that were appropriated by the Congress.

It is this setting which makes federal tax reduction both possible and necessary next year. I do not underestimate the obstacles which the Congress will face in enacting such legislation. No one will be satisfied. Everyone will have his own approach, his own bill and his own reductions. A high order of restraint and determination will be required if the "possible" is not to wait on the "perfect." But a nation capable of marshaling these qualities in any dramatic threat to our security is surely capable, as a great free society, of meeting a slower and more complex threat to our economic vitality. This nation can afford to reduce taxes, and perhaps even afford a temporary increase in the deficit — but we cannot afford to do nothing. For on the strength of our free economy rests the hope of all free nations.

I shall not fail that hope — for free men and free nations must prosper and they must prevail.[*]

---

[*] John F. Kennedy–Economic Club of New York Speech delivered Dec. 14, 1962 in New York, New York

CHAPTER NINETEEN
THE GRYPHON
INAUGURAL SPEECH

Our country - this great Republic - means nothing unless it means the triumph of a real democracy, the triumph of popular government, and, in the long run, of an economic system under which each man shall be guaranteed the opportunity to show the best that there is in him. That is why the history of America is now the central feature of the history of the World; for the World has set its face hopefully toward our democracy. Therefore, my fellow citizens, each one of you carries on your shoulders not only the burden of doing well for the sake of your country, but the burden of doing well and of seeing that this nation does well for the sake of mankind and free people everywhere.

In name we had the Declaration of Independence in 1776; but we gave the lie by our acts to the words of the Declaration of Independence; and words count for nothing except insofar as they represent acts. This is true everywhere; but it should be truest of all in political life. A broken promise is bad enough in private life. It is worse in the field of politics. No man is worth his salt in public life who makes on the stump a pledge which he does not keep after election; and, if he makes such a pledge and does not keep it, hunt him out of public life. I care for the great deeds of the past chiefly as spurs to drive us onward in the present. I speak of the men of the past partly that they may be honored by our praise of them, but more that they may serve as examples for the future.

Even in ordinary times there are very few of us who do not see the problems of life as through a glass, darkly; and when the glass is clouded by the murk of furious popular passion, the vision of the best and the bravest is dimmed.

It is of little use for us to pay lip-service to the mighty men of the past unless we sincerely endeavor to apply to the problems of the present precisely the qualities which in other crises enabled the men of that day to meet those crises. Under the lead of Abraham Lincoln, we, the American people, faced and solved the great problems of the nineteenth century. Now, however, these same good people nervously shrink from, or frantically denounce, those who are trying to meet the problems of today in the spirit which was accountable for the successful solution of the problems of Lincoln's time. Of that generation of men to whom we owe so much, the man to whom we owe most is, of course, Lincoln. Part of our debt to him is because he forecast our present struggle and saw the way out. He said:

"I hold that while man exists it is his duty to improve not only his own condition, but to assist in ameliorating mankind."

And again:

"Labor is prior to, and independent of, capital. Capital is only the fruit of labor, and could never have existed if labor had not first existed. Labor is the superior of capital, and deserves much the higher consideration."

If that remark was original with me, I should be even more strongly denounced as a Communist agitator than I shall be anyhow. It is Lincoln's. I am only quoting it; and that is one side; that is the side the capitalist should hear. Now, let the working man hear his side:

"Capital has its rights, which are as worthy of protection as any other rights. . . . Nor should this lead to a war upon the owners of property. Property is the fruit of labor; . . . property is desirable; is a positive good in the World."

And then as Lincoln himself said:

"Let not him who is houseless pull down the house of another, but let him work diligently and build one for himself, thus by example assuring that his own house shall be safe from violence when built."

It seems to me that, in these words, Lincoln took substantially the attitude that we ought to take now and in the future. He showed the proper sense of proportion in his relative estimates of capital and labor, of human rights and property rights. Above all, in this speech, as in many others, he taught a lesson in wise kindliness and charity; an indispensable lesson for us all today. But this wise kindliness and charity never weakened his arm or numbed his heart. We cannot afford weakly to blind ourselves to the actual conflicts which face us today. The issue is joined, and we must fight or fail.

In every wise struggle for human betterment, one of the main objects, and often the only object, has been to achieve in large measure equality of opportunity. In the struggle for this great end, nations rise from barbarism to civilization, and through it people press forward from one stage of enlightenment to the next. One of the chief factors in progress is the destruction of special privilege. The essence of any struggle for healthy liberty has always been, and must always be, to take from some one man or class of men the right to enjoy power, or wealth, or position, or immunity, which has not been earned by service to his or their fellows. That is what we strive for now.

At many stages in the advance of humanity, this conflict between the men who possess more than they have earned and the men who have earned more than they possess is the central condition of progress. In our day it appears as the struggle of freemen to gain and hold the right of self-government as against the special interests, who twist the methods of free government into machinery for defeating the popular will. At every stage, and under all circumstances, the essence of the struggle is to equalize opportunity, destroy privilege, and give to the life and citizenship of every individual the highest possible value both to himself and to the commonwealth.

Practical equality of opportunity for all citizens, when we achieve it, will have two great results. First, every man will have a fair chance to make of himself all that in him lies; to reach the highest point to which his capacities, unassisted by special privilege of his own and unhampered by the special privilege of others, can carry him, and to get for himself and his family substantially what he has earned. Second, equality of opportunity means that the commonwealth will get from every citizen the highest service of which he is capable. No man who carries the burden of the special privileges of another can give to the Country that service to which it is fairly entitled.

I stand for the square deal. But when I say that I am for the square deal, I mean not merely that I stand for fair play under the present rules of the game, but that I stand for having those rules changed so as to work for a more substantial equality of opportunity and of reward for equally good service. When I say I want a square deal for the poor man, I do not mean that I want a square deal for the man who remains poor because he has not got the energy to work for himself.

This means that our government, National and State, must be freed from the sinister influence or control of special interests. The great special business interests too often control and corrupt the men and methods of government for their own profit. We must drive the special interests out of politics. That is one of our tasks today. Every special interest is entitled to justice - full, fair, and complete - and, now, mind you, if there were any attempt by mob-violence to plunder and work harm to the special interest, whatever it may be, that I most dislike, and the wealthy man, whomsoever he may be, for whom I have the greatest contempt, I would fight for him. And you would too, if you were worth your salt. He should have justice. For every special interest is entitled to justice, but not one is entitled to a vote in Congress, to a voice on the bench, or to representation in any public office. The Constitution guarantees protection to property, and we must make that promise good. But it does not give the right of suffrage to any corporation.

The true friend of property, the true conservative, is he who insists that property shall be the servant and not the master of the Country; who insists that the creature of man's making shall be the servant and not the master of the man who made it. The citizens of the United States must effectively control the mighty commercial forces which they have called into being.

There can be no effective control of corporations while their political activity remains. To put an end to it will be neither a short nor an easy task, but it can be done.

We must have complete and effective publicity of corporate affairs, so that the people may know beyond peradventure whether the corporations obey the law and whether their management entitles them to the confidence of the public. It is necessary that laws should be passed to prohibit the use of corporate funds directly or indirectly for political purposes; it is still more necessary that such laws should be thoroughly enforced. Corporate expenditures for political purposes, and especially such expenditures by public-service corporations, have supplied one of the principal sources of corruption in our political affairs.

I believe that the officers, and, especially, the directors, of corporations should be held personally responsible when any corporation breaks the law.

There is a wide-spread belief among our people that the special interests are too influential. Probably this is true of both the big special interests and the little special interests. These methods have put a premium on selfishness, and, naturally, the selfish big interests have gotten more than their smaller, though equally selfish, brothers. The duty of Congress is to provide a method by which the interest of the whole people shall be all that receives consideration.

The absence of effective State, and, especially, national, restraint upon unfair money-getting has tended to create a small class of enormously wealthy and economically powerful men, whose chief object is to hold and increase their power. The prime need is to change the conditions which enable these men to accumulate power which it is not for the general welfare that they should hold or exercise. We grudge no man a fortune which represents his own power and sagacity, when exercised with entire regard to the welfare of his fellows. Again, my friends over there, take the lesson from your own experience. Not only did you not grudge, but you gloried in the promotion of the great generals who gained their promotion by leading their army to victory. So it is with us. We grudge no man a fortune in civil life if it is honorably obtained and well used. It is not even enough that it should have been gained without doing damage to the community. We should permit it to be gained only so long as the gaining represents benefit to the community. This, I know, implies a policy of a far more active governmental interference with social and economic conditions in this country than we have yet had, but I think we have got to face the fact that such an increase in governmental control is now necessary.

No man should receive a dollar unless that dollar has been fairly earned. Every dollar received should represent a dollar's worth of service rendered - not gambling in stocks, but service rendered. The really big fortune, the swollen fortune, by the mere fact of its size, acquires qualities which differentiate it in kind as well as in degree from what is possessed by men of relatively small means. Therefore, I believe in a graduated income tax on big fortunes, and in another tax which is far more easily collected and far more effective - a graduated inheritance tax on big fortunes, properly safeguarded against evasion, and increasing rapidly in amount with the size of the estate.

The people of the United States suffer from periodical financial panics to a degree substantially unknown to the other nations, which approach us in financial strength. There is no reason why we should suffer what they escape. It is of profound importance that our financial system should be promptly investigated, and so thoroughly and effectively revised as to make it certain that hereafter our currency will no longer fail at critical times to meet our needs.

It is hardly necessary for me to repeat that I believe in an efficient army and a navy large enough to secure for us abroad that respect which is the surest guaranty of peace. A word of special warning to my fellow citizens who are as progressive as I hope I am. I want them to keep up their interest in our international affairs; and I want them also continually to remember Uncle Sam's interests abroad. Justice and fair dealings among nations rest upon principles identical with those which control justice and fair dealing among the individuals of which nations are composed, with the vital exception that each nation must do its own part in international police work. If you get into trouble here, you can call for the police; but if Uncle Sam gets into trouble, he has got to be his own police-man, and I want to see him strong enough to encourage the peaceful aspirations of other people's in connection with us. I believe in national friendships and heartiest goodwill to all nations;

but national friendships, like those between men, must be founded on respect as well as on liking, on forbearance as well as upon trust. I should be heartily ashamed of any American who did not try to make the American government act as justly toward the other nations in international relations as he himself would act toward any individual in private relations. I should be heartily ashamed to see us wrong a weaker power, and I should hang my head forever if we tamely suffered wrong from a stronger power.

Of conservation, I shall speak more at length elsewhere. Conservation means development as much as it does protection. I recognize the right and duty of this generation to develop and use the natural resources of our land; but I do not recognize the right to waste them, or to rob, by wasteful use, the generations that come after us. I ask nothing of the nation except that it so behave as each farmer here behaves with reference to his own children. That farmer is a poor creature who skins the land and leaves it worthless to his children. The farmer is a good farmer who, having enabled the land to support himself and to provide for the education of his children, leaves it to them a little better than he found it himself. I believe the same thing of a nation.

Moreover, I believe that the natural resources must be used for the benefit of all our people, and not monopolized for the benefit of the few, and here again is another case in which I am accused of taking a revolutionary attitude. People forget now that one hundred years ago there were public men of good character who advocated the nation selling its public lands in great quantities, so that the nation could get the most money out of it, and giving it to the men who could cultivate it for their own uses. We took the proper democratic ground that the land should be granted in small sections to the men who were actually to till it and live on it. Now, with the water-power, with the forests, with the mines, we are brought face to face with the fact that there are many people who will go with us in conserving the resources only if they are to be allowed to exploit them for their benefit. That is one of the fundamental reasons why the special interests should be driven out of politics. Of all the questions which can come before this nation, short of the actual preservation of its existence in a great war, there is none which compares in importance with the great central task of leaving this land even a better land for our descendants than it is for us, and training them into a better race to inhabit the land and pass it on. Conservation is a great moral issue, for it involves the patriotic duty of insuring the safety and continuance of the nation.

Let me add that the health and vitality of our people are at least as well worth conserving as their forests, waters, lands, and minerals, and in this great work the national government must bear a most important part.

Nothing is more true than that excess of every kind is followed by reaction; a fact which should be pondered by reformer and reactionary alike. We are face to face with new conceptions of the relations of property to human welfare, chiefly because certain advocates of the rights of property as against the rights of men have been pushing their claims too far. The man who wrongly holds that every human right is secondary to his profit must now give way to the advocate of human welfare, who rightly maintains that every man holds his property subject to the general right of the community to regulate its use to whatever degree the public welfare may require it.

But I think we may go still further. The right to regulate the use of wealth in the public interest is universally admitted. Let us admit also the right to regulate the terms and conditions of labor, which is the chief element of wealth, directly in the interest of the common good. The fundamental thing to do for every man is to give him a chance to reach a place in which he will make the greatest possible contribution to the public welfare. Understand what I say there. Give him a chance, not push him up if he will not be pushed. Help any man who stumbles; if he lies down, it is a poor job to try to carry him; but if he is a worthy man, try your best to see that he gets a chance to show the worth that is in him. No man can be a good citizen unless he has a wage more than sufficient to cover the bare cost of living, and hours of labor short enough so after his day's work is done he will have time and energy to bear his share in the management of the community, to help in carrying the general load. We keep countless men from being good citizens by the conditions of life by which we surround them.

If I could ask but one thing of my fellow countrymen, my request would be that, whenever they go in for reform, they remember the two sides, and that they always exact justice from one side as much as from the other. I have small use for the public servant who can always see and denounce the corruption of the capitalist, but who cannot persuade himself, especially before election, to say a word about lawless mob-violence. And I have equally small use for the man, be he a judge on the bench or editor of a great paper, or wealthy and influential private citizen, who can see clearly enough and denounce the lawlessness of mob-violence, but whose eyes are closed so that he is blind when the question is one of corruption of business on a gigantic scale. Also, remember what I said about excess in reformer and reactionary alike. If the reactionary man, who thinks of nothing but the rights of property, could have his way, he would bring about a revolution; and one of my chief fears in connection with progress comes because I do not want to see our people, for lack of proper leadership, compelled to follow men whose intentions are excellent, but whose eyes are a little too wild to make it really safe to trust them.

National efficiency has many factors. It is a necessary result of the principle of conservation widely applied. In the end, it will determine our failure or success as a nation. National efficiency has to do, not only with natural resources and with men, but it is equally concerned with institutions. The State must be made efficient for the work which concerns only the people of the State; and the nation for that which concerns all the people.

I do not ask for the over centralization; but I do ask that we work in a spirit of broad and far-reaching nationalism where we work for what concerns our people as a whole. We are all Americans. Our common interests are as broad as the continent. The National Government belongs to the whole American people, and where the whole American people are interested, that interest can be guarded effectively only by the National Government. The betterment which we seek must be accomplished, I believe, mainly through the National Government.

The American people are right in demanding that New Economic Nationalism, without which we cannot hope to deal with new problems. The New Economic Nationalism puts the national need before sectional or personal advantage. It is impatient of the utter confusion that results from local legislatures attempting to treat national issues as local issues. It is still more impatient of the impotence which springs from over division of governmental powers, the impotence which makes it possible for local selfishness or for legal cunning, hired by wealthy special interests, to bring national activities to a deadlock. This New Economic Nationalism regards the executive power as the steward of the public welfare. It demands of the judiciary that it shall be interested primarily in human welfare rather than in property, just as it demands that the representative body shall represent all the people rather than any one class or section of the people.

I believe in shaping the ends of government to protect property as well as human welfare. Normally, and in the long run, the ends are the same; but whenever the alternative must be faced, I am for men and not for property. I am far from underestimating the importance of corporate profits; but I rank dividends below human character. Again, I do not have any sympathy with the reformer who says he does not care for corporate profits. Of course, economic welfare is necessary, for a man must pull his own weight and be able to support his family. I know well that the reformers must not bring upon the people economic ruin, or the reforms themselves will go down in the ruin. But we must be ready to face temporary disaster, whether or not brought on by those who will war against us to the knife. Those who oppose reform will do well to remember that ruin in its worst form is inevitable if our national life brings us nothing better than swollen fortunes for the few and the triumph in both politics and business of a sordid and selfish materialism.

If our political institutions were perfect, they would absolutely prevent the political domination of money in any part of our affairs. We need to make our political representatives more quickly and sensitively responsive to the people whose servants they are. More direct action by the people in their own affairs under proper safeguards is vitally necessary. The direct primary is a step in this direction, if it is associated with a corrupt-services act effective to prevent the advantage of the man willing, recklessly, and unscrupulously to spend money over his more honest competitor.

It is particularly important that all moneys received or expended for campaign purposes should be publicly accounted for, not only after election, but before election as well. Political action must be made simpler, easier, and freer from confusion for every citizen. I believe that the prompt removal of unfaithful or incompetent public servants should be made easy and sure in whatever way experience shall show to be most expedient in any given class of cases.

One of the fundamental necessities in a representative government such as ours is to make certain that the men to whom the people delegate their power shall serve the people by whom they are elected, and not the special interests. I believe that every national officer, elected or appointed, should be forbidden to perform any service or receive any compensation, directly or indirectly, from interstate corporations; and a similar provision could not fail to be useful within the States.

The object of government is the welfare of the people. The material progress and prosperity of a nation are desirable chiefly so long as they lead to the moral and material welfare of all good citizens. Just in proportion as the average man and woman are honest, capable of sound judgment and high ideals, active in public affairs,-but, first of all, sound in their home, and the father and mother of healthy children whom they bring up well, just so far, and no farther, we may count our civilization a success. We must have - I believe we have already - a genuine and permanent moral awakening, without which no wisdom of legislation or administration really means anything; and, on the other hand, we must try to secure the social and economic legislation without which any improvement due to purely moral agitation is necessarily evanescent. In the last analysis, therefore, vitally necessary though it was to have the right kind of organization and the right kind of leadership, it was even more vitally necessary that the average soldier should have the fighting edge, the right character. So it is in our civil life. No matter how honest and decent we are in our private lives, if we do not have the right kind of law and the right kind of administration of the law, we cannot go forward as a nation. That is imperative; but it must be an addition to, and not a substitute for, the qualities that make us good citizens. In the last analysis, the most important elements in any man's career must be the sum of those qualities which, in the aggregate, we speak of as character. If he has not got it, then no law that the wit of man can devise, no administration of the law by the boldest and strongest executive, will avail to help him. We must have the right kind of character - character that makes a man, first of all, a good man in the home, a good father, and a good husband - that makes a man a good neighbor. You must have that, and, then, in addition, you must have the kind of law and the kind of administration of the law which will give to those qualities in the private citizen the best possible chance for development. The prime problem of our nation is to get the right type of good citizenship, and, to get it, we must have progress, and our public men must be genuinely progressive.[*]

---

[*] Theodore Roosevelt – The New Nationalism Speech delivered August 31, 1910 Osawatomie, Kansas

CHAPTER TWENTY

ECONOMIC STRATEGY FOR THE NEW ADMINISTRATION

Sharp change in present economic policy is an absolute necessity. The problems of inflation, deflation and slow growth, of falling standards of living and declining productivity, of high government spending but an inadequate flow of funds for defense, of an almost endless litany of economic ills, large and small, are severe, they are not intractable. Having been produced by government policy, they can be redressed by a change in policy.

The new Gryphon Task Force reports that you commissioned during the campaign are now available. They contain an impressive array of concrete recommendations for action. More than that, the able people who served on the Task Forces are available to provide further detail and backup information to you or your designees. We all want to help and you can count on enthusiastic and conscientious effort from all of us in the Gryphon movement.

Your Coordinating Committee has reviewed the Task Force reports. With due allowance for some differences in view about particulars and relative importance, we have found that they offer a substantial base for action by you and the team you assemble. We focus here on guiding principles, on priorities and linkages among policy areas, and on the problem of getting action.

You have identified in the campaign the key issues and lines of policy necessary to restore hope and confidence in a better economic future:

- Reestablish stability in the purchasing power of the dollar.

- Achieve a widely-shared prosperity through real growth in jobs, investment, and productivity.

- Devote the resources needed for a strong defense, and accomplish the goal of releasing the creative forces of entrepreneurship, management, and labor by:

- Restraining government spending.

- Reducing the burden of taxation and regulation.

- Conducting monetary policy in a steady manner, directed toward eliminating inflation while avoiding deflation and recession.

This amounts to emphasis on fundamentals for the full four years, as the key to a flourishing economy.

GUIDING PRINCIPLES

The essence of good policy is good strategy. Some strategic principles can guide your new administration as it charts its course.

- **Timing and preparation are critical aspects of strategy.** The fertile moment may come suddenly and evaporate as quickly. The administration that is well prepared is ready to act when the time is ripe. The transition period and the early months of the new administration are a particularly fertile period. The opportunity to set the tone for your Administration must be seized by putting the fundamental policies into place immediately and decisively.

- **The need for a long-term point of view is essential to allow for the time, the coherence, and the predictability so necessary for success.** This long-term view is as important for day-to-day problem solving as for the making of large policy decisions. Most decisions in government are made in the process of responding to problems of the moment. The danger is that this daily fire fighting can lead the policy-maker farther and farther from his goals. A clear sense of guiding strategy makes it possible to move in the desired direction in the unending process of contending with issues of the day. Many failures of government can be traced to an attempt to solve problems piecemeal. The resulting patchwork of ad hoc solutions often makes such fundamental goals as military strength, price stability, and economic growth more difficult to achieve.

- **Central problems that your Administration must face are linked by their substance and their root causes.** Measures adopted to deal with one problem will inevitably have effects on others. It is as important to recognize these interrelationships as it is to recognize the individual problems themselves.

- **Consistency in policy is critical to effectiveness.** Individuals and business enterprises plan on a long-range basis. They need to have an environment in which they can conduct their affairs with confidence.

- **Specific policies as well as long-term strategy should be announced publicly.** The Administration should commit itself to their achievement, and should seek Congressional commitment to them as well. Then the public, as well as the government, knows what to expect.

- **The administration should be candid with the public.** It should not over-promise, especially with respect to the speed with which the policies adopted can achieve the desired results.

SEIZING THE INITIATIVE

The fundamental areas of economic strategy concern the budget, taxation, regulation, and monetary policy. Prompt action in each of these areas is essential to establish both your resolve and your capacity to achieve your goals.

BUDGET

Your most immediate concern upon assuming the duties of the President will be to convince the financial markets and the public at large that your cut-spending, decrease taxes, strong dollar anti-inflation policy is more than just rhetoric. The public, and especially the financial community, are skeptical and need a startling demonstration of resolve. Many question whether you are serious about a sizeable cut in budget outlays. Credible FY 2013 and 2014 budgets which do that clearly and unambiguously would evoke an extraordinary response in the financial markets, and set the stage for a successful assault on inflation and a decline in mortgage and other interest rates.

The FY 2013 Budget will be almost four months along by the time you take office and a FY 2014 Budget will have been submitted for consideration by the Congress. There are now estimates of alarming increases in these swollen budgets. Prompt and strong action is necessary if these budgets are to be brought under control, as they must be. The nation can no longer afford governmental business as usual. It has been over four years since the Senate has passed a budget; and the CBO says the Country is headed over a fiscal cliff.

The formal budget alone is far from the whole story, though it is visible and important. Off-budget financing and government guarantees mount and expand programs through the use of the government's borrowing capacity, draining the nation's resources without being adequately recorded in the formal spending totals. In addition, the mandating of private expenditures for government purposes has gained momentum as the spotlight has illuminated direct spending. These mandates are also a clear call by government on the nation's resources. Efforts to control spending should be comprehensive; otherwise, good work in one area will be negated in another. And these efforts should be part of the Administration's development of a long-term strategy for the detailed shape of the budget, four or more years into the future.

The Gryphon Task Force has identified an extensive and promising array of areas for potential savings, but it will be up to your Administration and the Congress to do the job. It takes top-notch people to do it. We recommend that:

- A Budget Director, permanent or pro tem, be chosen and set to work now.

- A small team from OMB be assembled explicitly to work with the newly designated Director.

- The Director's recommendations be a part of your discussion with Cabinet and sub-Cabinet appointees as these appointments are made.

- You should immediately name D.E. Carpenter as the new Commissioner of the IRS to send an immediate message that there will no longer be IRS raids, IRS collection activity, and that all tax penalties incurred between 2009 and 2012 will be immediately forgiven. That will send a very strong message to the markets.

Amendments calling for dramatic reductions in the FY 2013 Budget should be submitted to the Congress within the first week of your Administration. A thoroughly revised FY 2014 Budget provides even greater opportunities for large further reductions, and this budget should be submitted as soon as possible. You should call for immediate cuts in government agency payrolls as much as 80% of each agency should be cut.

Finally, it has become all too evident in recent years that current budget procedures are biased in an expansionary direction. The Congressional budget process defined by the Budget Act of 1974 and its subsequent amendments have failed to achieve their purpose of removing the "runaway" bias. We therefore recommend a presidential task force to develop new techniques which can help to rein in the growth of federal outlays and federal spending. It should re-examine the presidential line item veto, renewed presidential power to refrain from spending appropriated funds, and other initiatives to hold down spending. This task force should report to you within two months.

TAX POLICY

Tax policy is properly the province of your Secretary of the Treasury. The making of that appointment should have a high priority so that important work can go forward. The Gryphon Task Force provides the materials needed to pose the issues to you in concrete form and to translate your decisions into a proposal to the Congress. This proposal should be presented early in the new administration in tandem with other key elements of your economic program. It should embody the main thrust of tax policy for the whole of your first term, not simply for the year 2013. We consider that the key ingredients should be your proposals for the proposed cut in personal income tax rates, simplification and liberalization of business depreciation and a cut in effective taxes on capital gains by keeping the Bush tax cuts in place. Consistent with your proposals earlier this year, the effective date for these reductions should be January 1, 2013.

Other key proposals are tax incentives for the establishment of enterprise zones in the inner cities and such other items as tuition tax credits so people can tax deduct college tuition, and the elimination of all of the anti-growth tax penalties and regulations put in by the last administration. Once again, the biggest step is making Carpenter the new Commissioner of the IRS. Currently the Tax Code is one volume of Code and five volumes of Regulations. Each volume is larger than the King James Bible. The Code is Congress' fault. The five volumes of Regulations are the IRS's fault. Make Carpenter the new Commissioner and let him cut the Regulations to one volume.

REGULATION

The current regulatory overburden must be removed from the economy. Equally important, the flood of new and extremely burdensome regulations that the agencies are now issuing or planning to issue must be drastically curtailed. The Gryphon Task Force sets out the needed blueprint for personnel selection, immediate administrative action, and legislation. Again, the key to action is a knowledgeable and forceful individual to develop and coordinate strategy and to form a team to carry it out. Such an appointment should be made promptly, with the expectation that the effort would carry forward through the transition for at least a year into your Administration. Your appointee and his team should be located within the Executive Office of the President. Achieving regulatory reform will take informed, strong, and skillful work with the Congress, as well as with those in charge of departmental and agency regulatory efforts. The person heading up this effort will require your continued, wholehearted support.

Many of our economic problems today stem from the large and increasing proportion of economic decisions being made through the political process rather than the market process. An important step to demonstrate your determination to rely on markets would be the prompt end of wage and price guidelines and elimination of the Council on Wage and Price Stability, along with other federal agencies such as the Departments of Education, Energy, Labor and Commerce, along with terribly ineffective agencies like the Environmental Protection Agency. If not entirely eliminated, their budgets and payrolls should be immediately cut by 80%.

To advance the entire regulatory effort—both to galvanize public support and to strengthen the positions of Administration appointees—we urge you to issue a message on regulatory reform in tandem with the budget and tax messages. The message should call upon state and local governments to launch similar regulatory reform efforts—as a few have already done. The states and cities are necessarily cutting their budgets or facing bankruptcy. We cannot allow America to go over a fiscal cliff.

ENERGY

The battle between government regulation and the private market is nowhere more apparent than in energy, where the market has a decisive comparative advantage. Governmental intrusion into energy production and use provides a glaring example of how regulation costs us all dearly. Alternatives to imported oil exist here in the United States. As the Gryphon Task Force emphasizes, market pricing and market incentives will accelerate the development of these alternatives, just as surely as present regulations and the politicization of this field inhibit them. Its recommendations and the issues it poses for careful review cover the energy field in a comprehensive manner and deserve immediate attention. Look at North Dakota and Alaska. Look at the new uses of sugar-based, not corn-based, fuels.

We recommend, also, that you promptly exercise the discretion granted to the President to remove the price controls on crude oil and petroleum products and increase margin requirements to stop the speculators. This decisive action will eliminate at once the regulatory apparatus administering the entitlements program, and discourage continued efforts by special interests, to prevent or slow down decontrol and deregulation. Also, the Natural Gas Policy Act should be repealed so that all natural gas prices are decontrolled. These measures are particularly urgent because the uncertainty of our critical Middle East oil supplies, dramatized by the potential wars in the Middle East, makes it all the more necessary to get the earliest possible incentive effect of free market pricing.

The Department of Energy has become a large and unmanageable institution with a variety of programs ranging from essential to useless. The essential functions should be transferred and the Department eliminated. This should be the main task of your Secretary of Energy. The first year the payroll and budget should be cut by 80%, and the entire department eliminated by the second year of your first term.

MONETARY POLICY

A steady and moderate rate of monetary growth is an essential requirement both to control inflation and to provide a healthy environment for economic growth. We have not had such a policy. The rate of monetary growth declined sharply in the early months of 2012, and rose rapidly in recent months. These wide fluctuations are adversely affecting economic conditions and may continue to do so for some time.

The Gryphon Task Force emphasizes that the attainment of a proper monetary policy deserves the very highest priority and that such a monetary policy can be achieved by the Fed effectively using its existing powers. The Task Force also brings out the relationship of monetary policy to budgetary and other economic policies.

The Federal Reserve is an independent agency. However, independence should not mean lack of accountability for what it does. In practice, independence has not meant that the Federal Reserve is immune to Presidential and Congressional influence. The problem is how to assume accountability while preserving independence. We suggest that you:

- Request the Fed to state targets for monetary growth year by year for the next five years that in its opinion will end inflation. Influential members of relevant committees of Congress have already urged the Fed to specify such long-term targets.

- Assure the Fed that you will propose and fight for fiscal and other policies compatible with the elimination of inflation.

- Improve the procedures for coordinating Federal Reserve monetary policy with the economic policies of the Administration and the Congress and support Congressional efforts to monitor the Fed's performance and to recommend changes in the procedures that could improve performance.

With these fundamentals in place, the American people will respond. As the conviction grows that the policies will be sustained in a consistent manner over an extended period, the response will quicken. And a healthy U. S. economy, as the Gryphon Task Force states, will restore the credibility of our dollar on world markets, contribute significantly to smoother operation of the international economy, and enhance America's strength in the World. America needs a strong dollar and so does the World. We need to restore fiscal integrity as well as monetary integrity.

ORGANIZING FOR ACTION

The activities of a wide variety of departments, agencies, and other units of government within the Executive Branch impinge on economic policy. But the flow of economic events does not recognize organizational lines. The economy itself operates as a system in which constituent parts are linked, sometimes tightly. The combination of interwoven problems and disparate organizations means that, in the process of policy formulation and implementation, some people high in your administration must identify the central ideas and problems and devise a strategy and tactics for dealing with them. Your leadership is essential to this effort.

One arrangement that has worked well in the past is for the Secretary of Treasury to be the chief coordinator and spokesman on economic policy, domestic and international. To carry out this mandate effectively, the Secretary should be one of your key staff members as well as a departmental head with a White House title and office. Since economic developments are often closely related to security, the Secretary should be a member of the National Security Council. For this coordinating role, an Economic Policy Board, with comprehensive membership, should be established; it should meet regularly and be the avenue through which economic issues come to your Executive of the Cabinet and to your desk. The Council of Economic Advisers might suitably provide the secretariat for this group. None of this matters, however, if you do not have strong leadership at the post of the Commissioner of the IRS. Without a strong leader like Carpenter at the helm, tax reform is impossible. With Carpenter as Commissioner, he can reform the collection of taxes in such a way that the government gets more revenue with less taxpayer stress. The IRS under Carpenter will be a kinder, gentler IRS; taxpayer friendly; a system that works.

MAINTAINING A STEADY COURSE

Our final point is our most important one. The success of your economic policy will be a direct reflection of your ability to maintain a steady course over your full first term. Rough times will come and crises of one kind or another, some small, some of great moment, will arise. Sustained effort through these testing times means that public understanding and support are essential. Of equal and related importance is the understanding and support of the Congress.

This last task—gaining understanding and support of the Congress—is of crucial importance. As a result of the voting on November 6, the new Congress, we are convinced, will be more cooperative on economic and financial issues. That cooperation will be fostered if, during the transition, the Secretary of the Treasury (designate) consults intensively with key members of Congress on the design and implementation of your economic policies.

You have emphasized in your successful campaign precisely the strategy set forth in this document. In moving to implement it, you will be doing what the people voted for. Every effort must be made to maintain and broaden your base of support by improving public understanding and by close cooperation with the Congress. Cabinet officers and others in your administration can help in these tasks. Their ability to do so should be one important criterion in their selection.

At the end of the day, however, the burden of leadership falls on you: leadership to chart the course ahead; leadership to persuade that your course is the one to take; leadership to stay on course, whatever way political winds may blow. Through effective advocacy of the sharp changes so sorely needed, your leadership has brought us to this long-hoped-for opportunity at a critical moment for the nation. Your leadership can maintain this advocacy in the convincing manner necessary for a successful outcome.*

Arthur F. Burns

Milton Friedman

Alan Greenspan

Michael T. Halbouty

The Honorable Jack Kemp

James T. Lynn

Paul McCracken

William E. Simon

Charls E. Walker

Murray L. Weidenbaum

Caspar W. Weinberger

Walter B. Wriston

George P. Shultz, Chairman

---

* Excerpts taken from November 16, 1980 memo to President Elect Ronald Reagan entitled: *"Economic Strategy for the Reagan Administration."*

THE GRYPHON
POSTSCRIPT

This Book was written in the spirit of Thomas Paine's "*The American Crisis*", which was meant to be a wake up call to the apathetic majority of Colonists that if they valued their freedom, liberty, and their own pursuit of happiness they had better do something about the sad state of affairs that the Country was in at that time. Once again, we find ourselves in perilous times and our "Government of the People, by the People, and for the People" has been swallowed up by a bureaucratic monster known as Washington, D.C. Representatives with good intentions go there only to be swallowed up as well, while the People continue to suffer.

The same Justice Department that recently decided to not pursue charges against Goldman Sachs for their activities in the great financial crisis, had no problem mounting huge and expensive trials against baseball great Roger Clemens, Senator John Edwards, and number of young black men in Boston whose only crime was being caught with the same drugs that Bush (43) and the current President used before they became President. And no one is more guilty of lying to Congress and obstructing justice than Attorney General Eric Holder.

The Federal Budget must be cut. The next President must cut 80% of the federal work force in Washington, D.C. This President, however, has already hired 400,000 new Washington bureaucrats, 35,000 of them to be new "regulators" to oversee the more than 100,000 pages of new regulations.

The President also wants to hire 16,000 new IRS-CID Special Agents to monitor your healthcare. Governor LePage said it best: "America will now be less free." And before one criticizes Governor LePage's comments, wait until you take on the burden of not one, but two Government raids of your home or office and then let us know how you feel.

The IRS is out of control. The Treasury Inspector General says that the IRS is sending out as much as TWENTY BILLION DOLLARS in fraudulent tax refunds. At the same time, the Government has spent well over a Million dollars in legal fees trying to assess $5,000,000 in unconscionable and unconstitutional penalties against one small welfare benefit plan.

It is unbelievable that people watch the riots in Greece and believe it can't happen here. It will happen here if interest rates go up to 7% as they already are in Italy and Spain and once were here during the Carter and Reagan administrations. At 7%

all of the tax receipts will go to interest on the national debt; and nothing else.

People will riot in the streets when their Social Security checks, disability checks and unemployment checks all bounce. If you think people are leaving France now, wait until the first Millionaires are put on trial in America for "tax evasion" by the new IRS-CID. The new IRS-CID that knows how to bring a criminal case against honest businessmen but cannot seem to figure out that sending 20,000 tax refund checks to one address in Lansing, Michigan might be somewhat suspicious – something that should be investigated and prevented.

The Government wastes EIGHTY BILLION DOLLARS a year just in Medicare fraud. The easiest way to stop Medicare fraud is to have Medicare run by the BUCA monsters of Blue Cross, United Healthcare, CIGNA, and Aetna. The Government would pay the premiums, and the insurance carriers would provide the insurance. No one in Washington, D.C. builds bombers or aircraft carriers; why leave health insurance to the Government?

There are a number of people that have seen what is coming and have the courage to speak truth to power, though that might be the most dangerous thing to do in Society nowadays.

Most notably, Pete Peterson has funded David Walker and the Comeback America Initiative. Their websites, movies, and video clips should be required viewing for all Americans. Most importantly, they have created the American Financial Burden Barometer which shows the cost of the "off-balance sheet" benefits promised by the Government to be a staggering SEVENTY TRILLION DOLLARS. The Government that is helpless to trim One Hundred Billion Dollars from a SIXTEEN TRILLION DOLLAR national debt will have no hope of paying that kind of money in the future. There will be two more books on that subject after this, but you must wake up, study the problem, take a stand and do something. It does not matter whether you are a Republican or Democrat, if you care about America, you must become a Gryphon and support the candidates that think the way you do. If you care about America and its future, you must abide by the Gryphon Motto before it is too late:

"Lead, Follow, or Get Out of the Way."

– Thomas Paine

The following people are honorary Gryphons, as they have done their best to wake-up and shake-up America at a risk to their own popularity, and for the benefit of their fellow Americans:

- Roger Ailes – Fox News
- Erskine Bowles – Simpson-Bowles Commission
- Neil Cavuto – Author and Talk Show Host
- Jim Cramer – CNBC Talk Show Host
- Steve Forbes – Publisher
- Thomas Friedman – Author and New York Times Columnist
- Jim Grant – Publisher
- Sean Hannity – Author and Talk Show Host
- Joe Kernen – CNBC Anchor
- Larry Kudlow – CNBC Talk Show Host
- John McLaughlin – Talk Show Host
- Judge Napolitano – Author and Talk Show Host
- Bill O'Reilly – Author and Talk Show Host
- Pete Peterson – Author and Foundation Chairman
- Paul Ryan – Chairman of the House Budget Committee
- Joe Scarborough – Author and Talk Show Host
- Senator Alan Simpson – Simpson-Bowles Commission
- Andrew Ross Sorkin – Author and CNBC Anchor
- Ben Stein – Author
- John Stossel – Author and Talk Show Host
- David Walker – Former U.S. Comptroller General
- George Will – ABC News
- Mort Zuckerman – Publisher

Made in the USA
Lexington, KY
22 September 2012